World War II

An Enthralling Guide to the Second World War

Free limited time bonus

Stop for a moment. We have a free bonus set up for you. The problem is this: we forget 90% of everything that we read after 7 days. Crazy fact, right? Here's the solution: we've created a printable, 1-page pdf summary for this book that you're reading now. All you have to do to get your free pdf summary is to go to the following website: **https://livetolearn.lpages.co/enthrallinghistory/**

Once you do, it will be intuitive. Enjoy, and thank you!

Table of Contents

Introduction

More often than not, World War II is associated with the Holocaust and Hitler.

While this is not *untrue*, it is also not quite so simple. In the 1930s, by the time Adolf Hitler came along with a desire to conquer Europe, there were already many complex issues at play. The rise of Nazism and Hitler's power grab in Europe served to create the perfect storm, unleashing a chain of events that is now known as World War II.

Hundreds and thousands of books, articles, and journals have been written about the war, the Holocaust, and how the events from those six critical years continue to influence the world we live in today. With so much information available, it can be difficult to decipher the important points and events. The purpose of this book is to provide an accurate, concise, and comprehensive account of the key events of World War II in an easy-to-understand and enjoyable manner.

The book will begin with a brief look at how less than a quarter of a century after the end of one major global conflict, the world became embroiled in a second, perhaps far more disastrous one. It will also provide a clear understanding of the background to determine what led to the Second World War, as well as a look at the major events of the war.

Part One: The War Summarized (1939–1945)

Chapter 1: Invasion and Attack (1939–1941)

Starting as early as 1931, a global crisis was brewing. There were already rumblings of disquiet and tension in many parts of Asia and Europe. The United States withdrew completely from European affairs, choosing to take an isolationist stance.

However, when discussing World War II, the focus is often on Hitler's "rise and fall." As such, historically, World War II is officially said to have begun with Nazi Germany's invasion of Poland in 1939.

To understand why Hitler's Germany invaded Poland and why this act dragged most of the world's major players into the fray, we need to go back to 1919, to the end of the First World War.

After four years of war, on November 11th, 1918, an armistice was signed by the Germans and the Allied countries, officially bringing World War I to an end.

Brief Overview of World War I

World War I, also known as the Great War, started in 1914 with the assassination of Archduke Franz Ferdinand of Austria by Serbian nationalist Gavrilo Princip. With the support of German Kaiser Wilhelm II, war was declared against Serbia.

Serbia turned to Russia for help, and within a week, major European players were picking sides and joining the war. The Great War was fought between the Central Powers (Austria-Hungary, Bulgaria, Germany, and the Ottoman Empire) and the Allied Powers (France, Russia, Italy, Great Britain, Canada, United States, Romania, and Japan).

Technological advances in weapons and the use of poisonous gas led to a no-holds-bar type of war. The loss of lives was catastrophic. Over sixteen million civilians and soldiers lost their lives.

By 1918, it was evident the Central Powers were losing the war, and one by one, they began to surrender; Germany was the last hold-out. When it finally signed the armistice on November 11th, 1918, World War I officially came to an end.

Once the dust settled, it became apparent just how shocking the events of the war had been and what a trail of devastation it had left around the world. The carnage was so horrific and devastating that the Allies were determined that such a thing would never happen again.

Reshaping of Europe

After the war ended, four of the world's empires collapsed. As part of the peace talks, the Allies reshaped Europe and distributed territories that formally belonged to the Russian Empire, the German Empire, the Ottoman Empire, and the Austro-Hungarian Empire. Countries like Poland, Czechoslovakia, Hungary, Lithuania, and Turkey were created, while German colonies in the continent of Africa were divided between the Allies as part of the League of Nations' "mandates."

The redrawing of the European map would have far-reaching consequences and play a pivotal role in the Second World War.

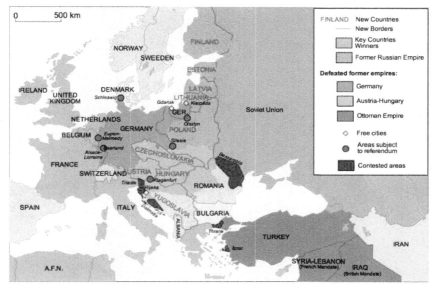

Map of Europe in 1923.

Source: Paris Peace Conference – Fluteflute;
https://en.wikipedia.org/wiki/File:Map_Europe_1923-en.svg

Divisions also happened in Asia, with Japan gaining control of Shandong Province. This was unacceptable to China since Shandong was part of its mainland. China also refused to sign the Treaty of Versailles.

What Was the Treaty of Versailles?

When the Allied leaders met in 1919 at the Paris Peace Conference, they decided the Great War had to be the "war to end all wars." The leaders expressed their intention of putting measures in place to prevent a future world war.

In June 1919, leaders from Great Britain, the United States, and France, among other nations, met at the Palace of Versailles in Paris and signed the Treaty of Versailles.

The four big leaders at the Treaty of Versailles

The treaty's main purpose was to outline the terms of peace at the end of the war. It was also designed to be punishing and humiliating for Germany. The treaty placed the blame of the war squarely on Germany's shoulders and imposed numerous penalties on the country.

For instance, Germany had to pay reparations, give up territories it had seized, and demilitarize, which limited Germany's land and naval forces (its air force was completely disbanded). The treaty did not try to understand or resolve the main issues or tensions that had led to the war. Instead, the Allies hoped severe punishments would ensure peace throughout Europe.

The Treaty of Versailles also set the stage for the creation of the League of Nations. The league was Woodrow Wilson's brainchild, and its purpose was to create an international organization that maintained world peace by mediating and resolving any conflicts before they got out of hand.

The League of Nations was a great idea in theory, but it suffered growing pains. The countries were not always good at putting aside their own self-interest, while key players, such as Germany, were forbidden from joining the organization. The League of Nations was disbanded during World War II (a war it had failed to prevent) and eventually evolved into what we know today as the United Nations.

Ironically, the Treaty of Versailles, the very thing designed to promote peace in Europe, indirectly led to the start of World War II since none of the long-simmering issues had actually been addressed or resolved.

The humiliating terms of the treaty crippled Germany's economy and caused growing resentment among the Germans. Many saw it as a punishment rather than an attempt at finding peace and harmony. This unrest gave Hitler the ideal platform to garner support for the Nazi Party and rise to power.

Causes of the Second World War

Anschluss

Trouble had been brewing in Europe long before the start of the Second World War. One of the issues at play was an *Anschluss*. The term refers to the creation of a "Greater Germany" where Austria and Germany would be united together.

After the end of WWI, the Republic of German-Austria wanted to unite with Germany but was not allowed to do so under the terms of the Treaty of Versailles. In fact, some of Austria's territories, like the Sudetenland, were taken away.

When Hitler, who was born in Austria, came to power, he dreamed of a unified Germany.

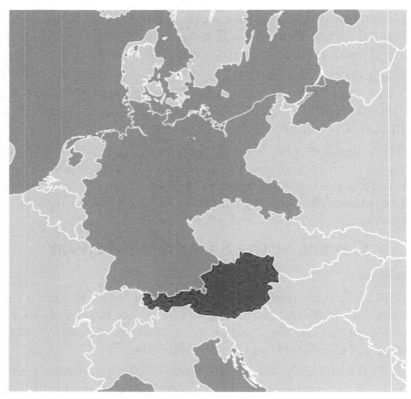

A map of the Anschluss, March 1938.

In 1920, after Hitler joined the National Socialist German Workers' Party (NSDAP), he stressed the importance of unifying "all Germans in the Greater Germany on the basis of the people's right to self-determination."[1] This sentiment and desire to unite Austria and Germany were reiterated by Hitler in his book, *Mein Kampf.*

Austria had also suffered greatly after WWI due to its unstable economy and high unemployment rate. A combination of Hitler coming into power and Nazi propaganda led to the Austrian Nazi Party's growing popularity in the country. The desire to join

---

[1] Hamann, Brigitte (2010). *Hitler's Vienna: A Portrait of the Tyrant as a Young Man.* Tauris Parke Paperbacks. p.107. ISBN 9781848852778.

Germany also grew as slogans like "One People, One Empire, One Leader" gained traction and swept through the nation.

Had things continued in this fashion, it is almost certain that the *Anschluss* would have happened. However, the Austrian Nazis began to use terrorist tactics to attack the Austrian government. They attempted a coup in July 1934. The coup failed, and power was taken by an authoritarian right-wing government.

In the meantime, during the 1930s, as Germany began rearming, Austria had become a rich source of both labor and raw materials. Germany desperately needed its resources. When Austrian Nazis began to make plans for a second coup, Austrian Chancellor Kurt von Schuschnigg set up a meeting with Hitler. He wanted to ensure Austria could remain an independent country. But under pressure from Hitler, he ended up appointing high-ranking Austrian Nazis to his government and calling a national vote to settle the matter of the *Anschluss.*

This was not enough for Hitler, though. Schuschnigg was faced with an ultimatum of an invasion, and he resigned from his position on March 11th, 1938. The national vote never took place.

Before resigning, Schuschnigg asked for help from countries like France, Italy, and Britain, but nobody wanted to interfere in the matter. During his resignation, Schuschnigg advised the Austrian people not to fight back against Germany should they advance into Austrian territory. He was arrested by the Nazis and taken away as a prisoner soon after.

On March 12th, German troops marched into a cheering Austria. Hitler established a Nazi government and declared *Anschluss* on March 13th. The country became a part of the Reich, and Austria ceased to be an independent nation.

As Hitler annexed Austria, the other powers did nothing, even though this was a direct violation of the Treaty of Versailles. Buoyed by his success, Hitler turned his sights on Czechoslovakia.

Invasion of the Czech Provinces

Within months of annexing Austria, it was clear to the world that Hitler's next move would be to occupy Czechoslovakia.

France and Great Britain had both promised to help the country; however, they did not wish to enter into another war. They instead decided to compromise with Germany to maintain the peace.

After several back-and-forth messages between France, Germany, Britain, and Italy, the Sudetenland was handed over to Germany under the Munich Agreement. In exchange, Hitler pledged not to wage war in Europe. Czechoslovakia was not consulted in the matter and was told it could accept the decision or take on the German Army alone.

Ethnic Germans in the Sudetenland greet German troops with the Nazi salute.

Czechoslovakia had no choice but to accept. Great Britain and France believed they had averted a crisis and prevented another war. They were wrong. Not even six months later, on March 15th, 1939, Hitler violated the terms of the Munich Agreement and sent his troops into Bohemia and Moravia, annexing the provinces to the Reich.

Once again, the powers in Europe said nothing. They made some faint protests, but there were no real repercussions for Germany from breaking the Munich Agreement.

Invasion of Poland

Hitler's ultimate dream and goal was to create one unified German Empire and conquer Europe. Six months after annexing the rest of Czechoslovakia and receiving little more than a slap on the wrist, Hitler invaded Poland on September 1ˢᵗ, 1939.

Poland had a weak military, and Hitler knew if he moved quickly, he could easily gain control of the country. He correctly assumed that none of the European powers would intervene in time to stop him.

When Hitler invaded Poland, the Soviet Union was already on his side. The two nations had made a secret agreement called the Hitler-Stalin Pact, Nazi-Soviet Pact, or Molotov-Ribbentrop Pact (named after the foreign ministers of the countries who signed the pact). The pact essentially guaranteed that neither country would declare war on the other. It also included some secret provisions to divide up some of the smaller countries, including Poland, between them.

Hitler's troops invaded Poland soon after the pact was signed, and the Soviet Union made no protests. Instead, Stalin began preparing his own troops for an invasion of Poland.

And now the world leaders began to get a little worried.

Blitzkrieg

When Germany invaded Poland, the country put up a valiant effort to resist Hitler's troops. However, the under-equipped and unprepared Polish forces were no match for Germany's calculated bombarding and blitzkrieg strategy. Within a month of German forces advancing on Warsaw, the Polish army surrendered.

The blitzkrieg approach is how Hitler intended to win the war in Europe. This approach basically meant immobilizing the enemy as quickly as possible via whatever means necessary. For Hitler's troops, this involved the Luftwaffe (the German air force) relentlessly bombing the country they were invading so that communication lines, railroads, important landmarks, offices, and other key areas were completely destroyed and rendered useless.

A German dive bomber.

https://commons.wikimedia.org/wiki/File:Henschel_Hs_123_in_flight.jpg

The bombing was followed by tanks and troops moving in to take whatever they could. The final step was for the infantry to come through and do a final sweep, removing any final obstacles along the way.

Within days of an invasion, the troops were ordered to set up a base to control the country and gather intelligence. The security forces were given orders to get rid of anyone who opposed Nazi ideology. Concentration camps were also quickly set up.

By 1939, the Nazis had become something of an expert in the creation of concentration camps. The very first one, Dachau, had been built six years prior, soon after Hitler became chancellor of Germany. Although that camp was used for political prisoners, it would later be used as a model for the other concentration camps that were built during the Holocaust, most of which were built for a very different purpose.

The concentration camps were managed by the SS (the Schutzstaffel or "Protection Squad"). Within a day of his troops invading Poland, Hitler had already organized SS regiments whose sole purpose was to ignite fear and obedience among the Polish people.

While Germany took control and annexed eastern Poland, Stalin sent his troops in to annex western Poland.

With the invasion of Poland, Hitler had finally overstepped. Great Britain and France, which had done everything they could to stay out of another conflict, declared war on Germany on September 3rd, 1939.

World War II had begun.

Beginning of the Holocaust

When German forces took over Poland, Nazi ideologies and beliefs began to be enforced almost immediately. Hundreds of thousands of Polish people were sent away, allowing ethnic Germans to settle in their homes instead, while Nazi policies began to be introduced.

On November 23rd, 1939, the Nazi governor general in Poland decreed that Jewish people had to wear a white armband with a blue Star of David on it. This helped the Nazis identify and separate the Jews from the rest of the population.

An armband seller in the Warsaw ghetto.
https://www.timesofisrael.com/new-book-dredges-up-warsaw-ghetto-police-who-sent-fellow-jews-to-their-deaths/

Jewish people were also enlisted to work in camps as slaves. As the war progressed and Hitler's power grew, the fate of the Jewish people would become far worse. The Nazi Party would devise the "Final Solution" to solve the Jewish problem.

Hitler's European Conquest: An Overview

After Poland, Hitler and his troops were like a war machine, rapidly sweeping through parts of Europe and invading and conquering country after country. And they found victory every time.

Poland was defeated and occupied within weeks in September 1939. The following year in April 1940, Hitler took over Denmark and Norway just as easily. A month later, Belgium, Luxembourg, the Netherlands, and France were occupied by Nazi forces.

When Hitler tried to invade Great Britain, the British navy protected the English Channel while the Royal Air Force defended the skies. Hitler's German forces were unable to defeat either and had to turn back.

After abandoning his plans to invade Great Britain, Hitler set his sights elsewhere instead. In April 1941, he took Yugoslavia and Greece. Two months after this, Hitler suddenly and without provocation decided to go after the Soviet Union.

This would be the beginning of the end.

But before we get to that, let's take a closer look at some key battles and events.

The Battle of Dunkirk

A small coastal town in northern France near the French-Belgian border, Dunkirk (or Dunkerque) had been the site of many battles long before Hitler's troops invaded. However, it is most associated with WW2 and the critical role it played in the war effort. The Battle of Dunkirk was fought for less than two weeks and signified the end of the "phony war." It would be a turning point in the war for the Allies.

The seven months between September 1939 and April 1940, when Hitler was rapidly moving around Europe collecting countries like trophies with little fighting, is often referred to as the "phony war." Even though war had been declared, the fighting hadn't started in earnest.

This changed as soon as Hitler began a blitzkrieg attack on Belgium, the Netherlands, and Luxembourg. It didn't take his forces long to occupy all three countries, and within a period of three weeks, Hitler had taken over all three.

France was expecting to be invaded next, so it was prepared. However, Hitler sent his troops not along the Maginot Line (a line made by the French consisting of concrete barriers and fortifications) but by the Somme Valley, near the English Channel.

The French were not expecting this.

As the German forces continued to advance, the British and French forces were pushed back and left trapped on the French coast. It soon became apparent to the Allied forces that they had to evacuate Dunkirk since they had no hope of winning against the German forces.

Thankfully, Hitler ordered his troops to stop advancing because he was worried about a counterattack from the Allies. By stopping his troops, he inadvertently gave the British and French forces enough time to prepare for an evacuation.

A couple of days later, when Hitler urged his troops forward again, plans were already in place for Operation Dynamo. Despite the vicious German bombing attacks on the shores of Dunkirk, the Allied forces were able to evacuate over 338,000 troops.

Approximately ninety thousand troops were left behind. They were unable to push back the German offensive. The German forces continued with their blitzkrieg invasion. Dunkirk surrendered to German troops on June 4th, and the country collapsed on June 22nd.

Why was Dunkirk so important to the Allied forces when they had been so soundly defeated? Even though the Allies did not win the battle, it was seen as a success and referred to as the "Miracle at Dunkirk" because the vast majority of the troops had been rescued.

Hitler believed the blitzkrieg attack of France would lead to Great Britain bowing out of the war, clearing the path for him to take over Europe. However, this did not happen.

The Battle of Dunkirk was a symbolic win for the Allies and strengthened their resolve, determination, and perseverance to continue the war effort.

The Battle of Britain

Following the fall of France, Hitler believed it would only be a matter of weeks before he gained control of Great Britain as well. In fact, he believed the war was over and that he had won. When

Great Britain did not crumble or bow out of the war, instead making it very clear the war would continue, Hitler started to reconsider his options.

But before this big loss, Hitler was dreaming of a quick victory. On July 16th, 1940, Hitler declared his intention to invade the country and started preparing for it. The invasion was given the name Operation Sea Lion.

Despite all of the German Army's previous victories and successes across Europe, it was woefully unprepared for the invasion. The German forces had not received any training; they did not have enough aircraft and had very little experience with crossing a sea while waging a war. German admirals felt their best option for a successful invasion would be to attack via the skies.

Hermann Göring, one of Hitler's most trusted military leaders, felt confident the Luftwaffe could take on the Royal Air Force (RAF) through an air offensive. They decided the goal would be to simply wear down the country's air defenses and deplete its resources until German forces could gain control.

On July 10th, the Germans started bomber attacks on ports and convoys. This continued for nearly a month until August 13th, when the main offensive called "Eagle Attack" began. Air bases, factories, and radar stations were all targets. Germany had larger troops and more fighters than England. But the British had Chain Home, a far superior radar system. Chain Home allowed for early warnings of Luftwaffe attacks, which allowed the British forces to be prepared.

Britain also had better aircraft. The twin-engine German bombers didn't have the capability to render utter destruction, and their dive bombers were easy to shoot down. Some of their other aircraft couldn't fly long distances. The RAF did not have these issues.

The inferiority in the Germans' equipment led them to lose almost half their aircraft within a month of invading Britain, while the British only lost about a third. Germany was also carrying out the invasion in an inconsistent manner and dropping bombs in civilian areas of London. The Germans said this was done accidentally, but Britain, nonetheless, retaliated by bombing Berlin, much to Hitler's fury.

Following the raid on Berlin, Hitler ordered the Luftwaffe to start attacking other cities. For nearly two months, London was subjected to nightly raids. But Britain held strong, and by the middle of September, German bombers were being shot down at an alarming rate.

The RAF was so deadly and precise that the Luftwaffe changed tactics and began to carry out their attacks at night only. These attacks were known as the Blitz and resulted in tens of thousands of civilian deaths.

German forces made no major headway or advancement through these raids. They were unable to dominate the British skies, and it quickly became clear to Hitler that he was fighting a losing battle.

In early September, he decided to cut his losses and announced the invasion of Britain would be pushed back by a few weeks. By October, he had decided to halt the operation since winter was coming.

The German troops withdrew, and by the time spring arrived, Hitler was looking at Russia with renewed interest. Plans to invade England were put on the back burner.

Whether Germany wanted to admit it or not, Great Britain had soundly defeated them.

Invasion of Russia

Even though Hitler had signed a non-aggression pact with Stalin prior to invading Poland, he never intended to honor the pact and only saw it as a temporary measure while he focused elsewhere. Getting rid of the communist Soviet Union and expanding his empire into Eastern Europe had long been cherished dreams for Hitler. In fact, going back as early as the 1920s, some core Nazi ideologies included eradicating communism and seizing land in Russia for German settlement.

The invasion of the Soviet Union was codenamed Operation Barbarossa. It was an enormous military operation involving over 3,500,000 troops. The order for the invasion had been planned well in advance, and Hitler signed the directive in December 1940.

The following year, on June 22nd, 1941, German troops officially invaded Russia.

The invasion took Russia completely by surprise. For months, the Allies had warned Russia that this was coming their way, but they did not believe it. And it did not take Hitler long to destroy Russia's air force, which was stationed on the ground.

A significant portion of the Soviet Army was trapped by German forces and forced to surrender. The army was followed by the Einsatzgruppen (SS death squads), whose role was to identify threats, eliminate the threat, gather intelligence, and establish intelligence networks.

The Einsatzgruppen was also known as "mobile killing squads." They played a key role in the extermination of Jews. Mass shootings were conducted by the mobile killing units. Anyone who was viewed as a threat to Nazi Germany was shot dead by the SS. While mass killings took place, millions of other citizens were deliberately starved by the Nazis and eventually died due to mistreatment.

The Soviet Union began to be used as a place to send German Jews and eventually evolved into the "Final Solution."

Although the Soviet Union was initially overwhelmed by Hitler's invasion, the country did not collapse. Halfway through August 1941, they started to push back, making the invasion anything but an easy victory.

Nonetheless, the German forces continued to make strides. By December, they had finally made it to the outskirts of Moscow. But they were unprepared for the Russian winter. Hitler had expected to gain full control of the Soviet Union by fall and had not planned ahead for the cold months. As a result, the army was exhausted, ill-equipped, and half-starved. When Russia launched its counterattack, it was able to easily drive the Germans away from Moscow.

The Tripartite Act

While Hitler was focused on invading European countries, Japan and Italy were busy waging wars and signing agreements to benefit their interests.

Several years before invading Poland, on October 25th, 1936, Germany and Italy signed the Rome-Berlin Axis. In November of the same year, Japan signed the Anti-Comintern Pact and joined the Axis powers. This pact was basically an anti-communist pact and was also signed by Italy in 1937. The pact fell apart when Hitler and Stalin signed their non-aggression pact in 1939 so that Germany could invade Poland without Soviet interference.

In 1940, the Axis powers (Germany, Italy, and Japan) held a meeting in Berlin with the intention of creating a defense alliance. This became the Tripartite Pact.

Under the terms of the Tripartite Pact, each country had to "assist one another with all political, economic and military means." The attack had to be by a power "at present not involved in the European War or in the Sino-Japanese Conflict."

It was deliberately worded in this manner to warn the United States to stay out of the war. Some other European countries, like Hungary, Croatia, and Romania, would go on to sign the pact as well, but most of them were forced or threatened to do so.

For the most part, the Tripartite Pact served no real purpose since the Axis countries were each pursuing their own interests and agendas. It was only invoked once, after Japan bombed Pearl Harbor on December 7th, 1941.

Why Japan Bombed Pearl Harbor

Japan attacked the United States partially due to mounting tensions and partially as a preventative measure. While Europe was busy fighting with each other, Japan was quietly working away at building its own empire near the turn of the 20th century.

After waging two wars with great success and fighting in WWI with the Allies, Japan now had bigger dreams. The biggest challenge to the country's expansion was the lack of natural resources.

The solution was simple: invade Manchuria. The League of Nations frowned upon this invasion of China, so Japan withdrew from the league.

Following the invasion and capture of Manchuria and an altercation on the Marco Polo Bridge near Beijing, Japan and China were embroiled in the Sino-Japanese War. The Japanese forces quickly captured Nanjing (Nanking). Over a period of six weeks, they carried out mass killings and other atrocities against the Chinese living there.

While the United States had steadfastly refused to engage in any more European conflicts, it wanted to put a stop to these atrocities and put a stop to Japan's plans of global expansion. The US started to impose economic sanctions on the country, including embargoes on oil and other goods.

After months of negotiations, Japan and Washington were unable to resolve their disputes or accept each other's terms. The US maintained its decision to continue with the economic sanctions, which Japan found unacceptable. It was further incensed by the US sticking its nose in and interfering with Asian affairs. Japan knew it needed to do something to retaliate, especially if it wanted to be taken seriously as a major player.

Since the US had such a powerful military, Japan knew its only shot at winning would be to take the US by surprise. The decision was made to bomb Pearl Harbor and destroy the US Pacific Fleet in Hawaii. It was seen as an easy target, and the United States would not be expecting an attack there. Japan hoped the preventive action would stop the US from getting in Japan's way as it continued to advance in Southeast Asia and other overseas territories. The Japanese also hoped to negotiate a peace treaty once they had the upper hand.

Early on the morning of Sunday, December 7th, 1941, at 7:48 a.m., the Japanese began attacking the US base. Three hundred fifty-three Imperial Japanese aircraft were launched from half a dozen aircraft carriers in two separate waves.

A photo of the attack on Pearl Harbor.

https://commons.wikimedia.org/wiki/File:Pearl_harbour.png

Over 180 US aircraft were destroyed, almost twenty ships were either destroyed or damaged, and thousands of Americans were killed and wounded.

Initially, Japan believed its attack was a success. But the Japanese failed to completely destroy the Pacific Fleet since they missed important ammunition sites, oil tanks, and other facilities. Furthermore, not even one US aircraft carrier was at the base at the time of the attack. The attack ultimately turned the tide of the war.

On December 8th, both the United States and Great Britain declared war on Japan and officially entered the war.

Between December 11th and 13th, Germany and its Axis partners declared war against the United States.

The "phony war" was well and truly over. The early stages of Hitler advancing upon Poland and other European countries would seem like child's play compared to the bloodshed and violence yet to come.

With all the major powers of the world declaring war on each other, all bets were off. The world once again found itself plunged right back into the same kind of global conflict the Allies had tried so hard to prevent twenty-five years prior.

Chapter 2: The War Expands 1941–1943

War in the Pacific

Hitler's dream of a European conquest turned into a global war once Japan and the United States entered the picture. Japan was on the side of the Axis, while the US sided with the Allies.

To understand how these countries came to join the war, we have to go back to the early 1930s, a time when there were already grumblings of dissatisfaction quietly spreading around the world.

The conflicts in Asia began years before Hitler's invasion of Poland. They began, in part, because Japan needed raw materials like fuel to keep its industries running. So, on September 18th, 1931, Japan invaded Mukden, a city in the Chinese province of Manchuria.

The Japanese military moved forward ruthlessly and was no match for the Chinese army. By September 21st, with help from Korea, the Japanese army quickly began to take control of the entire province of Manchuria. In a matter of three months, Japanese troops could be found all over the province. The occupation of Manchuria continued until 1945.

The resistance from China was minimal, as Chiang Kai-shek, a Chinese military leader and politician, was busy pursuing his own agenda of gaining control of China. He advised the army not to resist and left the matter up to the League of Nations. The league's investigation found that Japan had behaved in an aggressive manner, but they did not place any sanctions on the country. Japan retaliated by withdrawing its membership from the League of Nations. In 1937, Japan attacked China, beginning the Second Sino-Japanese War.

Second Sino-Japanese War (1937–1945)

When China finally began to resist Japanese expansion by mounting a full-scale resistance, an undeclared war broke out between the two countries.

Historically, the war is divided into three separate phases:

1) Japan's invasion of Manchuria and rapid expansion from 1931 to 1938

2) A stalemate from 1938 to 1944

3) Involvement of the Allies during the Second World War and Japan's surrender

When the United States started to impose sanctions on Japan as a way of curtailing its plans for expansion, Japan sought to gain the upper hand by attacking Pearl Harbor. While there were many factors at play behind the scenes, Pearl Harbor ultimately led to both countries entering the world war on a bigger scale.

The Battle of Midway (June 4th, 1942, to June 7th, 1942)

Japan saw the United States as a hindrance on its path to expanding its control over East Asia. The Japanese desperately wanted to remove US influence from the Pacific. By attacking Pearl Harbor, they were hoping to do just that. With one swift move, Japan could cripple the US military base and set itself up as the dominant power in the region.

Unfortunately, while Pearl Harbor had been a successful campaign for Japan, it also resulted in the US entering the war.

Undeterred, Japan continued its efforts to claim dominance in the Pacific. This led to the Battle of the Coral Sea in May 1942, where they were soundly turned away by the US Navy.

Believing this to be a minor setback, the commander of the Japanese Navy was determined to have another success like Pearl Harbor. Six months after attacking Pearl Harbor, the Japanese forces were planning another sneak attack, this time on Midway Island, which sat between the two countries. The Japanese hoped this would destroy the remainder of the US Navy located in the Pacific.

They expected this to be a quick and efficient victory; unfortunately, it would become the beginning of the end for Japan's expansion goals.

What Japan did not know was that starting in 1942, US Navy cryptanalysts were secretly breaking the Japanese Navy's JN-25b code. They were privy to messages and communications sent by Japan and knew about Japan's plans to attack a location it named "AF" in the US.

The cryptanalysts suspected the location might be the base at Midway, and this was confirmed when the Americans set a trap for Japan. A fake message was sent out saying that Midway was "short of fresh water."[2] A code was sent out by Japan saying that "AF was short of fresh water." By breaking this code, the US Navy was able to confirm the location. They were also confident the attack would occur on June 4th or 5th.

As a result of breaking these codes, when Japanese aircraft carriers swooped over Midway to begin their attack, the US was ready. Carrier forces were hidden away, and when the Japanese aircraft headed back to refuel and get more arms, the US Navy attacked the fleet and destroyed them.

Only one Japanese carrier survived: the *Hiryu*. It was able to retaliate and cause considerable damage to one of the US ships. Later that day, a scout plane found the *Hiryu* and attacked. The *Hiryu* burned and eventually sank.

An all-out war between the two countries broke out over the next few days as they continued to attack each other relentlessly. The Japanese suffered heavy losses, losing over three thousand men,

[2] "The Battle of Midway." https://www.nationalww2museum.org/war/articles/battle-midway

while the US lost just under four hundred men.

Mikuma at Midway.
https://commons.wikimedia.org/wiki/File:Japanese_heavy_cruiser_Mikuma_sinking_o n_6_June_1942_(80-G-414422).jpg

Although it was fought over just a few days, the Battle of Midway played a very critical role in the war. The US emerged victorious and halted Japan's plans to expand control in the Pacific, leaving the Axis power in a weakened position.

Executive Order 9066

Following the attack on Pearl Harbor, it was not surprising that anti-Japanese sentiment was on the rise. Some of the largest Japanese communities were based in close proximity to the Pacific coast, which was also where many American war assets were located. These communities and Japanese Americans began to be viewed with deep suspicion and mistrust by other Americans.

Military commanders felt nervous about having the "enemy" so close and asked Henry Stimson, the Secretary of War, to do something about it. Henry Stimson turned to the president, Franklin Delano Roosevelt (FDR), who issued Executive Order 9066.

Without making specific mention of the Japanese, President Roosevelt issued the executive order on February 19th, 1942, essentially giving the secretary of war carte blanche to move or evacuate any individual or groups of individuals the government deemed a threat to America's national security.

Even though Japan was not mentioned, the directive was clear. Under this order, Japanese Americans' rights under the Fifth Amendment were denied and revoked. They received no trials and were not given due process. It didn't matter if the individual was a citizen or American by birth. Simply being of Japanese descent was enough.

Within days of the order being issued, over 1,500 leaders in the Japanese community were arrested. Thousands of other Japanese-born individuals had their assets frozen by the government. In southern California, Japanese immigrants began to be forced out of their homes with only a few belongings.

Proclamations establishing military areas were issued, and it was determined that any and all individuals with a Japanese background would have to leave California. The War Relocation Authority was created with the signing of Executive Order 9102 on March 18th, 1942. This was signed to allow a civilian-led agency to help move the immigrants.

Camps were set up across the country to house them. The first group was transferred to the Manzanar War Relocation Center, which was located in the desert in California. The center basically consisted of a series of barracks surrounded by barbed wire. It was guarded by armed troops and would become home to the displaced Japanese for three years.

In total, ten internment camps were set up, and over 120,000 Japanese Americans were incarcerated at these camps.

For all intents and purposes, they had become prisoners and were kept at these camps until the end of the war. Many people's lives were uprooted forever, while others lost everything they had ever worked for.

On December 18th, 1944, nearly two years after the signing of Executive Order 9066, the United States Supreme Court found the government did not have the right to detain any American citizens without just cause. The ruling, while a positive step, did not change the situation of the incarcerated Japanese overnight. It would take over four years for the government to remove everyone from the internment camps.

Three years after the war ended, the Evacuation Claims Act was signed by US President Harry Truman. The act allowed Japanese Americans who had lost their properties and belongings during the relocation to submit claims.

It's deeply unsettling that while fighting the Nazis and the atrocities they were committing against Jewish people, the US government approved the internment of Japanese Americans. Some of the similarities are difficult to ignore. In fact, these centers were initially referred to as "concentration camps." However, after Hitler's concentration camps were discovered, the term was no longer used in America. What's equally shocking is that it would take over three decades for the order to be fully rescinded! It was done so formally on February 16th, 1976, by President Gerald Ford.

The injustice faced by Japanese Americans was officially recognized in 1988 when the Civil Liberties Act was passed by Congress. Approximately $1.6 billion was paid out in reparations to the victims or their surviving families.

War Expands to Africa

Abyssinia (Present-day Ethiopia)

The Second World War even touched Africa! As Hitler moved around Europe with his expansion plans, Benito Mussolini, the fascist dictator in Italy, was considering his next steps with an eye on Africa.

Mussolini decided to expand his empire in Africa and boost Italy's image. In 1895, Italy had unsuccessfully tried to invade and occupy Abyssinia (present-day Ethiopia), so Mussolini wanted to try for it again, planning to add it to East African territories already under Italian control.

In October 1935, Mussolini attacked Abyssinia, igniting a conflict in North Africa and eventually bringing Africa into World War II. While the League of Nations rebuked his actions, no meaningful sanctions or penalties were imposed. Mussolini had anticipated this reaction and continued with the invasion. By June of the following year, the capital of Addis Ababa was successfully captured by Italy, and the Italian ruler was named king of Abyssinia.

The League of Nations continued to do nothing save to make a few protests. Meanwhile, Italy continued to control and occupy Abyssinia until 1941, when British and South African troops liberated the country while fighting in the Second World War.

First Battle of El-Alamein (July 1st–July 27th, 1942)

Another country in Africa to become embroiled in World War II was Egypt.

Egypt became involved in 1940 when Italy decided to invade one of its colonies, Libya. Italy was not successful in its invasion; however, they were saved from defeat by its ally, Germany.

A German officer named Erwin Rommel was charged with leading Germany's Afrika Korps during the war.

A photo of Erwin Rommel.

The Afrika Korps was established by Hitler in January of 1941 in order to help Mussolini maintain control of the territories he had gained in North Africa. According to Hitler, Germany had to provide support to Italy for "strategic, political, and psychological reasons."[3]

The British Army was already engaged in a number of battles and skirmishes with the Royal Italian Army in Egypt, and in a matter of months, Italian troops had mostly been pushed out of the country.

So, to help his friend and ally, Hitler commanded General Rommel to go to Libya and handle the situation. Unfortunately, taking control proved more difficult than anticipated. Rommel met resistance from Italian troops who didn't like taking orders from a German officer. They also had a difficult time adjusting to the weather. In short, they were not as organized or as prepared as they should have been.

While Rommel was in Libya, British forces pushed him into a defensive position. However, this was short-lived.

Hitler's gamble initially paid off, and the Axis forces, under Rommel's leadership, were able to recapture Libya. In early 1942, Axis troops defeated British troops at Gazala and took over Tobruk. By using the Panzer divisions, Rommel forced the British to retreat into Egypt.

The First Battle of El-Alamein would take place between July 1st and July 27th, 1942. Rommel's arrival saved the Italian troops from total defeat, and the Axis powers felt confident about their victory. Britain's naval base, which was located in Alexandria, Egypt, was only sixty miles away, and they had no doubts that they would be able to capture it. Mussolini and Hitler felt it was only a matter of time before Egypt became a part of their empire.

However, the British troops received supplies from the United States and troops from South Africa, India, and New Zealand, assuring the Axis powers did not get their anticipated victory. Instead, the First Battle of El-Alamein resulted in a stalemate, with

---

[3] "German General Rommel Arrives in Africa." https://www.history.com/this-day-in-history/rommel-in-africa

the Axis once again on the defensive.

The Second Battle of El-Alamein (October 23rd--November 11th, 1942)

The Allies were determined to bring an end to the Axis powers' ambitions in the Middle East. They took the summer to regroup and plan under the newly appointed Lieutenant General Bernard Montgomery.

A photo of Bernard Montgomery.

British Prime Minister Winston Churchill wanted the battle to be fought immediately. However, General Montgomery wanted to take it slow and steady and ensure his troops were adequately prepared, both physically and mentally.

Montgomery had 190,000 men under him. These men came from places like Greece, France, Poland, and British colonies, to name a few. He wanted to ensure everyone was trained properly and had all the necessary equipment and reinforcements.

By late October, Montgomery was feeling confident and ready to head out. He had trained a powerful and capable Allied force and was now eager to go head-to-head with the brilliant and infamous Erwin Rommel, who earned the nickname "Desert Fox" because of his skilled and cunning tactics on the battlefield.

Three months after the First Battle of El-Alamein ended in a stalemate, the second battle began. On October 23rd, 1942, artillery barrages were unleashed by the Allied forces.

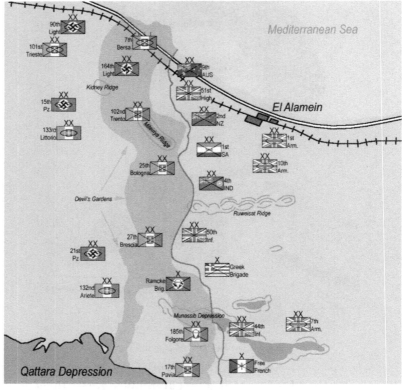

Deployment of forces before the second battle began.

The first phase of the battle was called Operation Lightfoot, and it began with the creation of two channels through minefields. The Allied forces used these channels to advance on the Axis forces and begin fighting them in a relentless assault.

Although the Allied forces were able to hold up successfully against counterattacks from the Axis forces, they did meet with some challenges when tanks got stuck in the minefield corridors. But the Allied troops held on, and the final attack was launched a week after the battle began on November 1ˢᵗ.

By November 2ⁿᵈ, Rommel told Hitler he had lost the battle. By November 4ᵗʰ, the Axis troops were retreating. In just over ten days, the battle was over. It had resulted in a resounding defeat for the Italian and German troops.

The Second Battle of El-Alamein would prove to be critical. In fact, the battle is historically viewed as the climax of what was happening in North Africa between the Axis and the Allies. It was a very clear and definitive victory for the Allies. After years of setbacks and defeats on the battlefield, they had finally found their groove.

Symbolically, the battle would signal the beginning of the end for the Axis powers. It provided a great boost in morale for the Allies and was heavily celebrated. Montgomery's reputation was also firmly cemented after this victory, something he capitalized on heavily.

The Atlantic Conference (August 14ᵗʰ, 1941)

While these battles were being fought across Europe and North Africa, the United States was still keeping itself out of the war, preferring to maintain a neutral stance.

While publicly there was no question about who the US sided with in the war, the country was reluctant to formally enter it. The American people were very firmly against getting involved in something they viewed as a "European problem." This was a sentiment Franklin Delano Roosevelt was hoping to change with the Atlantic Charter.

On August 9ᵗʰ and 10ᵗʰ, 1941, British Prime Minister Winston Churchill and American President Franklin D. Roosevelt met on a US warship called *Augusta*, which was docked in Placentia Bay off the coast of Newfoundland, Canada. Over a period of several days, they discussed what they wanted and envisioned for a post-war world.

Roosevelt and Churchill on the quarterdeck of HMS Prince of Wales during the conference.

One of Churchill's main goals in attending these meetings was to convince the US to join the war effort or at the very least increase the amount of aid and support to the United Kingdom. Roosevelt was hoping for the same. He hoped the public would see why it was important for the US to enter the war and help out the Allies.

To both leaders' disappointment, the Atlantic Charter meetings did not result in the US formally declaring war. The American people were still not behind the move, and FDR was reluctant to declare war without greater support. The US would join the war, but that would not happen until a few months later with Japan's attack on Pearl Harbor. However, even without formally joining the war, the US was already looking toward the future and what the world would like after the war ended.

There were doubts in the minds of some of the Allied nations that Hitler would be defeated. The US and the UK wanted to be prepared for the post-war world, placing a strong emphasis on global peace. What the Atlantic Charter *did* do was present a united front to the world, which was something the Axis powers did not take kindly to.

Following Roosevelt and Churchill's meeting, a joint declaration was released by them on August 14th, 1941. The declaration was called the Atlantic Charter, and this pivotal policy provided an overview of what they hoped to achieve from this war.

The Atlantic Charter.

Eight points were highlighted in the charter. They are as follows:

1) The US or the UK would not seek to gain any additional territories or aggrandizement;

2) Any changes or adjustments to territories could not be made without the consent of citizens and the peoples living on the land in question;

3) Self-determination of nations, meaning every person had the right to choose the type of government they wanted; this would be respected by the UK and the US;

4) The UK and the US would help countries gain equal access to raw materials and trade;

5) Encourage global collaboration to improve economic progress amongst all countries, promote safety and security, and maintain a similar labor standard;

6) Destroy the Nazis and look at how all countries and their citizens could live in peace;

7) This peace should also include peace on the seas so ships could travel without fear of attack;

8) Any country tagged as a potential aggressor had to be dealt with and disarmed.

The document and the eight points were approved by the Allied countries.

The Atlantic Charter was a significant piece of legislation since it would later (January 1ˢᵗ, 1942) be signed by the countries as the Declaration of the United Nations. It became the foundation of what we know today as the United Nations.

In addition to providing the foundation for the United Nations, the Atlantic Charter also heavily influenced the post-war fight for independence for many colonies and inspired international agreements, such as the General Agreement on Tariffs and Trade (GATT).

Siege of Leningrad (September 8th, 1941– January 27th, 1944)

With the Holocaust and the plight of the Jewish population often emphasized when discussing World War II, the atrocities suffered by the Soviets at the hands of Hitler's armies are often forgotten.

One of the most surprising events from the war—though maybe it should *not* have been surprising—was Hitler's decision to launch Operation Barbarossa. This was the codename for Hitler's invasion of the Soviet Union, which, as you know, was a German ally.

On June 22nd, 1941, Germany's Army Group North, which was made up of over three million troops, swarmed through the Soviet Union and began attacking. The invasion effectively ended the non-aggression pact Hitler had signed with Stalin a few years earlier, in 1939.

Historians widely believe that Hitler had always intended to invade the Soviet Union and that the signed pact had simply been a stalling mechanism.

Hitler was keen to capture Leningrad for strategic reasons. As the former capital of Russia, Leningrad was politically symbolic. Home to over six hundred factories, including arms factories, the potential for industrial output in Leningrad was enormous. Also, the city played a very important role as a base for the Soviet Navy along the Baltic Sea.

Within a matter of weeks, the Red Army was defeated, leading to the start of the long and infamous Siege of Leningrad (present-day St. Petersburg).

When the Axis forces first entered the Soviet Union, their main target was Leningrad. The plan was to encircle it with the help of Finnish allies. The two armies worked efficiently and methodically. The town of Chudovo was reached by August 20th, while Tallinn was taken eight days later. Rail links were severed whenever necessary.

While the Germans attacked Leningrad from the south, the Finnish forces invaded from the north. Their goal was to encircle Leningrad and cut it off completely from the rest of the Soviet Union.

By August 31ˢᵗ, the town of Mga was seized by the Germans. Shlisselburg was captured a mere week later. Mga had the last rail connection to Leningrad, while Shlisselburg had the last roadway open to Leningrad. Both connections were promptly severed by German troops as they took over the cities.

After that, Leningrad's only connection to the world beyond was through a water route near Lake Ladoga. This route was used by the Soviets to bring whatever food, supplies, and fuel they could get their hands on into the city. Relentless bombing and shelling over Leningrad by the Luftwaffe killed and wounded over fifty thousand civilians.

By late September, Hitler had decided that his army would settle at Leningrad. But what was he going to do with the people inside the city? Surrender was not an option, and he commanded that all such requests had to be denied. Accepting the population's surrender would mean having to ensure their safe passage to another city, keep them safe from harm, or worse, feed them. Lack of food was a significant problem faced by the Germans and the people of Leningrad alike. In addition, he could save his men by starving out a population he deemed "undesirable."

Hitler had no desire or interest in dealing with the citizens of Leningrad. Initially, he wanted to raze the city to the ground. In a memo, he stated his desire to *"...encircle the city and level it to the ground by means of artillery bombardment."*[1] However, the fighting was tougher than he had anticipated. The best way to deal with people at Leningrad, he decided, was simply to wait for them to die of starvation.

During the winter of 1941/42, known as the "Hungry Winter" in Leningrad, Hitler's wish began to come true. An average of one hundred thousand people died of starvation *per month*, with most deaths occurring during the first winter. The lack of food had become so extreme that people ate anything that could be considered edible, including petroleum jelly and animals. Cases of cannibalism also rose.

---

[1] "The Siege of Leningrad." https://www.history.com/news/the-siege-of-leningrad#:~:text=On%20September%208%2C%201941%2C%20German,the%20lives%20of%20800%2C000%20civilians.

Coupled with the food shortage, the people of Leningrad also had to deal with the extreme cold. In early 1942, the Soviets managed to get nearly half a million civilians out of Leningrad through the water route of Lake Ladoga.

Once the winter passed, Leningrad focused on surviving and defying the Germans in any way possible. Food and supplies continued to be an ongoing problem; however, the people banded together to try and clean up the city and even planted gardens. When Dimitri Shostakovich performed a symphony he had written at the start of the siege, Leningrad acted as the host. The concert could be heard all over Leningrad on loudspeakers, which were defiantly positioned toward the German camps.

Since the beginning of the siege, the Red Army had tried on numerous occasions to break through Germany's blockade. Each attempt had been unsuccessful and resulted in the loss of many lives. By early 1943, however, things began to look up for Leningrad.

At the start of the year, the Red Army tasted a tiny slice of victory when they managed to take a land bridge away from the German troops. The bridge was used to build a special railway, and by the time 1943 rolled to an end, millions of tons of food and other vital necessities had been brought into Leningrad. The factories were up and running and doing extremely well, producing tons of ammunition and arms.

Even though Germany continued to bomb the city, Leningrad was feeling more positive. The city was determined to fight back and reclaim what was theirs.

Just a couple of months later, in early 1944, the tide had definitely turned. It was becoming increasingly clear the Axis powers were fighting a losing battle.

The Red Army managed to mobilize over one million men and launched an offensive against the German troops, forcing them to retreat. Hitler's Army Group North soon had to follow suit. Eight hundred seventy-two days after the siege, Leningrad was finally free!

But the price of freedom had been steep.

It is estimated that approximately 800,000 civilians were killed during the siege, with some numbers going over a million. The

Siege of Leningrad is one of the longest blockades in history. Due to the number of deaths, some say it was one of the deadliest sieges. In fact, some historians argue that if we consider the atrocities that occurred during the siege and the number of lives lost, the siege should be classified as genocide.

Due to heavy censorship by the Soviet Union, the true extent of what happened during the siege may never be known. While many details were released after the end of the Cold War, there is much that remains unknown.

The Battle of Stalingrad (August 23rd, 1942– February 2nd, 1943)

While Leningrad was under siege and completely blocked off from the rest of Russia, the Red Army was continuing its fight elsewhere in the country.

As the Germans continued to overrun the Soviet Union, Russian troops were able to successfully stop them from taking over Stalingrad. Like Leningrad, Stalingrad was an industrial city and would have been a huge boon for Hitler and his army if they had managed to capture it.

Unfortunately for the Germans, they failed.

The Battle of Stalingrad was hugely successful, and many agree that it was one of the greatest battles fought during the war.

During the battle, the Russian troops stopped the Germans from advancing. In a war marked by several significant, history-making victories, this was one of them. The outcome of the battle helped to turn the tide of the war against the Axis powers.

The Battle of Stalingrad will be discussed in more detail in the next chapter, where we will examine how, after a string of losses, the war suddenly shifted in favor of the Allies.

When we look at some of the key events that took place between 1941 and 1943, it's clear it was a very stressful period. Within two years of Poland being invaded, Hitler and his Nazis had become a global problem. Altercations, existing tensions, and political leaders' ambitions to create empires all came to a head during this time and turned a European skirmish into a world war.

The period between 1941 and 1943 was especially nerve-wracking since nobody had any way of predicting which way the war would go. It often seemed as if victory for Hitler and his allies was assured. If he had won some of these key battles, where would we be today?

Chapter 3: The Turning Tide — Resistance and Surrender 1943–1945

The period between 1941 and 1943 was riddled with anxiety for the Allies, but when the Allied forces masterfully turned things around, it was like a domino effect. When one enemy was defeated, another swiftly followed.

The Allies were winning battle after battle, tasting victory at nearly every corner.

One of the major turning points in the war for the Allies was the fall of the Italian regime and Benito Mussolini's resignation. Knocking down this fascist regime was a significant victory and left Germany in a weaker position.

Benito Mussolini

Long before Hitler came into the picture, fascism was already in existence in Europe. Since 1925, Italy had been ruled by a fascist dictator named Benito Mussolini, also known as Il Duce.

A photograph of Benito Mussolini.

Hitler greatly admired Mussolini. Many Nazi ideologies were based on Mussolini's fascist ideologies. Mussolini, for his part, helped the Nazi Party by providing financial help and allowing Nazi troops to train with his squad of soldiers, the Blackshirts.

The two countries and leaders shared a lot in common and were military allies. However, their relationship was not always the strongest.

While Mussolini publicly applauded Hitler's rise to power in the early 1930s, he did not think much of him and even expressed his disapproval of Hitler's ideas and beliefs. While Mussolini firmly believed in the superiority of "white Europeans," he did not have the same type of hatred for Jewish people as Hitler did. Mussolini also did not agree with Hitler's extreme views on Aryan supremacy.

Mussolini and Hitler's first meeting, which took place in the summer of 1934 in Venice, did not go well. Neither Hitler nor Mussolini understood each other well due to a language barrier (Mussolini refused to use a translator), and both of them came away from the meeting disappointed in each other.

However, if there was one thing both men understood well was the power of propaganda. A carefully curated image of solidarity and friendship was presented to the world, making everyone believe the two were much closer than they actually were.

Slowly, over time, the two men did forge something akin to a friendship. More importantly, even as they prioritized their own agendas, they became allies and partners.

For example, when Italy invaded Ethiopia in 1935, Germany became one of the first countries to recognize and acknowledge Italy's legitimacy over the country. When Hitler terminated Germany's membership in the League of Nations, Mussolini also pulled out as a show of support.

As time went on, Hitler's influence on Mussolini grew to the point where Mussolini issued a decree in July 1938 called the Manifesto of Race. This manifesto was geared toward Jewish Italians. It called for them to lose their Italian citizenship, which meant they had to leave their government positions and could not be employed by the Italian government.

Pact of Friendship – May 1939

The relationship between Italy and Germany was further solidified in May 1939 when Hitler and Mussolini signed the Pact of Friendship or "Pact of Steel."

In the agreement, both nations pledged to help each other with economic and military support if one became engaged in a war. The pact also included a secret agreement that they would prepare for a war in Europe. However, they also agreed not to do anything to trigger a war until at least 1943.

Of course, Hitler broke this part of the pact in a matter of months. He had already set the ball in motion to start a second world war.

When Hitler invaded Poland in September of 1939, Mussolini chose to remain neutral, going against the pact. He refused to support Hitler or the Nazis by saying Italy simply wasn't ready for a war.

Mussolini's Resignation and Italy's Surrender

By the time Italy joined the war almost a year later in June 1940, Hitler's troops had invaded and occupied almost all of Western Europe. So, Mussolini set his sights elsewhere, namely in Africa.

Almost from the beginning, Italy began to fail, doing so first in Africa, where they were defeated and ousted by the Allies. In 1940, Italy also invaded Greece. Hitler did not approve of the move, thinking it to be a mistake. Not wanting his ally to lose face, Hitler came swooping in, overtaking the Allied forces in Greece. He pinned the failure of Operation Barbarossa on Mussolini.

In July 1943, the Allies invaded Sicily, and the fascist regime collapsed. On the night of July 24th, the Grand Council of Fascism met under cover of darkness to figure out Italy's next steps.

Dino Grandi, Italy's former Minister of Justice, turned on Mussolini, expressing his frustration with Mussolini's leadership style. Grandi proposed that some of Il Duce's powers as leader be transferred to King Victor Emmanuel III. The motion passed quickly, and Mussolini was forced by the Grand Council to resign. He did so on July 25th, 1943.

After his resignation, Mussolini, who was somewhat in a daze over everything that had happened, went to keep his regularly scheduled meeting with King Victor Emmanuel, where he was advised that Pietro Badoglio would now be taking over the duties as prime minister.

Mussolini had nothing to say about any of this. After he left his meeting, the police arrested him. Mussolini quietly accepted his fate and did not protest when he was sent to Ponza. Ponza was an island that Mussolini had used for decades to imprison his enemies. And Ponza would now become his prison.

Mussolini's fall from power had been swift and rather pitiful. As word spread around the country about Il Duce's arrest, a sense of relief washed over the population. Nobody, not even the most die-hard fascist, fought to save him. Italy's chief concern was where to go from there. Should they continue fighting alongside Hitler and the Nazis? Or should they wave the white flag?

Ultimately, Italy made the decision to bow out of the war, and it surrendered unconditionally to the Allies on September 8ᵗʰ, 1943.

Less than two years after the surrender, when the war ended, Mussolini was executed.

Tehran Conference (November 18th– December 1st, 1943)

Historically, the United States and the Soviet Union have not always had the warmest relationship, and leading up to the Second World War, the relationship between them was quite strained. The idea of an alliance or cooperation was laughable. The relationship had worsened significantly after Joseph Stalin signed the non-aggression pact with Germany in 1939.

However, Hitler had since turned on Stalin. Faced with the idea of destruction at the hands of a common enemy, the countries came together to forge a partnership.

This alliance between the "Big Three" is commonly known as the Tehran Conference.

By the time the US joined the war, the British were already providing assistance and support to the Russians, so it was only natural for the Soviet Union to become an ally of the United States.

From November 18ᵗʰ to December 1ˢᵗ, 1943, US President Franklin D. Roosevelt, British Prime Minister Churchill, and Soviet Premier Joseph Stalin met in Tehran, Iran, to discuss military strategies that would help them invade Nazi-occupied France and defeat both Germany and Japan.

The Tehran Conference was a significant moment in history as it was the first conference to be held between the three most powerful Allied leaders during World War II.

The three leaders in Tehran: Stalin, Roosevelt, and Churchill (left to right).

https://commons.wikimedia.org/wiki/File:Tehran_Conference,_1943.jpg

During the conference, key decisions about the post-war world were made. Of course, each leader had his own objectives, but they were all united in their determination to get rid of Hitler once and for all.

At the conference, the Western Allies agreed to invade France and launch a western offensive against Nazi Germany. The three leaders agreed to support Reza Shah's government in Iran while Stalin promised support to Turkey if the two countries, which had remained neutral during the war, would pledge to enter the war on the side of the Allies.

It was decided at the conference that the invasion of France by the American and British troops would take place in May 1944. Once Nazi Germany was defeated, the Soviet Union would then join in to attack Japan.

There can be no doubt that without the Soviet Union's cooperation and help, the Allies would have had a much harder time winning the war. It is widely believed and accepted that without the Soviet Union, World War II would have had a very different outcome. Russia was at the forefront of some of the most significant battles, pushing the Nazis back from further advancing. Hitler's army was far more ruthless and savage with the Russians than with the Western powers.

Among the three big powers, the Soviet Union suffered the most casualties, with approximately twenty-six million Soviets dying during the war. Just over eleven million of them were soldiers. President Dwight D. Eisenhower himself wrote in his memoir that when visiting Russia in 1945 he "did not see a house standing between the western borders of the country and the area around Moscow...so many numbers of women, children, and old men had been killed that the Russian Government would never be able to estimate the total."[5]

The country also paid a steep price in the sheer amount of industrial capacity lost to the Nazis. Because of the Cold War that followed and the continued tensions with Russia after, it's often easy to forget the critical role the Soviet Union played during the war. But it is a role that must be acknowledged.

The Tehran Conference was a highly significant event. The Siege of Leningrad ended within a month of the meeting, and the outcome of the discussions played a major role in the liberation of France and steered the war in the right direction.

End of the Siege of Leningrad

We covered the siege of Leningrad in a prior chapter, but since it was such an important part in turning the tide of the war, we will briefly sum it up here. The siege of Leningrad began in September 1941, but Soviet forces made repeated attempts to break through the blockade. However, with all roads and railway connections leading out of Leningrad cut off and destroyed, Soviet forces had a very difficult time making progress.

By cutting all connections, the Nazis ensured that civilians would have no access to food or other resources. What they were not able to touch, however, was Lake Ladoga. It became the only route available to the Soviet forces. It was especially useful in the winter when the lake froze over, creating an actual road.

---

[5] Tharoor, Ishaan. "Don't Forget How the Soviet Union Saved the World from Hitler." https://www.washingtonpost.com/news/worldviews/wp/2015/05/08/dont-forget-how-the-soviet-union-saved-the-world-from-hitler/

This route was also known as the "Road of Life," as it allowed the evacuation of nearly one million civilians and literally saved the lives of the remaining people in Leningrad since troops were able to pass along some food and other necessities.

The Soviet troops' determination to get through slowly began to pay off. By early 1943, they had managed to breach the German encirclement and were able to bring in more food and supplies to the civilians. And on January 12th, 1944, after the successful launch of a counteroffensive, they were finally able to force the Germans to retreat.

Soviet forces kept pushing forward until the German troops ended up on the outskirts of the city. The siege of Leningrad was over at last.

Often referred to as the 900-day siege, the Siege of Leningrad lasted for a total of 872 days. Approximately one million lives were lost, and hundreds of thousands were uprooted and displaced forever, torn away from everything they had ever known. The bittersweet victory was celebrated with a gun salute as civilians poured out onto the streets, laughing, crying, and singing.

For the remaining civilians of Leningrad, the nightmare was finally over.

In 1945, the city received the Order of Lenin, an award from the government to highlight their bravery, endurance, and fighting spirit. Twenty years later, in 1965, the city was also given the title of "Hero City."

The Liberation of Paris

One of the most enduring images of victory during World War II is soldiers on the beaches of Normandy. When we read about winning the war, it is invariably tied to D-Day or the Battle of Normandy.

While D-Day was by no means the only decisive battle, it has become synonymous with winning the war. This is, in part, because the liberation of Paris *was* a huge deal. When the Germans were finally ousted from Paris, it truly felt like the end was in sight.

Germany invaded France soon after the start of the war, so rescuing the country from Nazi occupation was like seeing the light at the end of a very long and dark tunnel. And for the French, who had been occupied by the Nazis for nearly the entire duration of the war and forced to submit to the rule of Hitler's army, it *was* freedom.

Whether the war was over yet or not, they were finally free.

During the Battle of France, which took place between May 10th to June 25th, 1940, Germany invaded France, Belgium, Luxembourg, and the Netherlands. In just a matter of six weeks, German troops drove out the British forces. By June 14th, 1940, Paris had fallen. After the invasion and occupation of the city, the French Third Republic had little choice but to dissolve itself. They surrendered to Germany on June 22nd, 1940.

Power was handed over to Marshal Philippe Pétain, a soldier and hero of the First World War. Under Pétain, an armistice was signed with Germany. An authoritarian government was established in the town of Vichy, France.

French General Charles de Gaulle, however, refused to bow down to the Germans. Days before the country's surrender, he fled to the UK, where he received support and assistance from the British government.

Charles de Gaulle

While the puppet government in Vichy was "running" the country, the exiled Charles de Gaulle was busy setting up his own government called Free France, which was funded by the British government.

Free France refused to accept the puppet government and was determined to resist and fight back. They urged and encouraged the people of France to put up a fight against the German invasion. Charles de Gaulle, in the meantime, sought support from the French colonies. It took several years, but by 1943, French Chad and other French colonies had pledged their support to him.

Over four years of Nazi occupation followed the invasion of France. The Allies' top priority was getting rid of the Germans from the Soviet Union and France. During the Tehran Conference, the liberation of Paris became one of the key points of discussion.

The Allied Army

After the conference, it was decided that American and British troops would mount a cross-Channel invasion into France and try to get the Nazis out.

Hitler had long been anticipating such a move and put Erwin Rommel in charge of reinforcing France and building an Atlantic Wall. The Atlantic Wall was meant to act as a 2,400-mile-long line of defense along the French coastline. It would be filled with obstacles, mines, pillboxes, and bunkers. However, the Nazis had neither the money nor the resources to undertake such a massive project, so they concentrated on fortifying existing ports instead.

While the Allies had been talking about a cross-Channel attack since 1942, the lack of resources and a clear strategy kept getting it delayed. It was clear to the Allies that the best way forward was to stretch the German forces thin. This could be achieved by opening up the Western Front in Europe. The tricky part was deciding which location should be targeted and, most importantly, when.

Preparations for the attack only began in earnest in December 1943, with a record number of American troops landing in the United Kingdom. British soldiers had been undergoing intense training for the invasion since 1942 and felt fully prepared.

As they planned for the invasion, the future president of the United States, Dwight D. Eisenhower, was appointed as commander of the Supreme Headquarters Allied Expeditionary Force (SHAEF). He would work with Bernard Montgomery, the man who had fought against and defeated Rommel back in Africa.

General Dwight D. Eisenhower.

Eisenhower's chief of staff was an American named Walter Bedell Smith. His other subordinates, Air Chief Marshal Arthur Tedder, Admiral Bertram Ramsay, and Air Chief Marshal Trafford Leigh-Mallory, were all British. Charles de Gaulle's Free France also sent a delegate named Marie-Pierre Koenig to act as a liaison between de Gaulle and the Allied Expeditionary Force.

By the spring of 1944, over 1.5 million American soldiers were in Britain, ready for action. Lieutenant General J. C. H. Lee was responsible for overseeing logistics. By May 1944, he had 6,500 ships and landing crafts ready. The landing crafts would assist with the landing of approximately 200,000 vehicles and 600,000 tons of supplies during the first few weeks of the invasion.

Air support was also given a key role in the campaign to combat the Luftwaffe. The Allies had over thirteen thousand bomber, fighter, and transport aircraft. Prior to the actual invasion, Allied troops dropped more than 195,000 tons of bombs at key locations in France, including German airfields, military bases, and rail centers. The aircraft destroyed all the bridges crossing the Seine and Loire Rivers.

These preliminary attacks were very important since they helped to completely isolate the area that would be invaded by the Allies from the rest of the country. It was also meant to deceive the Germans and make them believe Allied troops would land in Pas-de-Calais instead of Normandy. The Allies did so by dropping the bulk of their bombs in the wrong area.

An added bonus of the air campaign was that it left the German troops feeling a little rattled. They were forced to concede that the Allied troops were far superior when it came to aircraft.

It had taken the Allies years to prepare for the invasion, but it was time well spent because they were extremely well prepared. Aside from launching a very successful air campaign, the Allies had also become adept at decrypting German codes and thus had a fairly good idea of where Nazi forces were situated and what their next steps would be.

One of the more brilliant moves by the Allies was creating phantom armies using false radio transmissions. They based the phantom army at Dover, England, directly across from Pas-de-Calais.

Montgomery's Plan

D-Day was an extremely complicated military operation. It required precise coordination, meticulous planning, and a dash of luck.

While Eisenhower was assigned to direct SHAEF, General Bernard Montgomery was the ground commander responsible for leading the 21st Army Group and organizing Operation Overlord, the codename given for the Battle of Normandy. The 21st Army Group was made up of Allied ground forces and was the group that would put Operation Overlord into action.

What's interesting and rather amusing about Montgomery's plan is that it was laid out on *one* solitary sheet of paper. He marked the document as "Most Secret" on the very top and wrote, "The key note of everything to be SIMPLICITY," at the very bottom.

In the end, his battle plan *was* rather simple, as so many brilliant things are.

For the invasion, Montgomery requested five divisions to land at five different beaches instead of three. He also asked to have the landing area include the Orne River.

Each of the five beaches was given a codename. They were as follows:

- Utah
- Omaha
- Gold
- Juno
- Sword

The plan had two parts to it. The first part, called NEPTUNE, required Allied troops to cross the English Channel, land on the beaches, and provide support with gunfire. The second part of the plan, called OVERLORD, was the actual invasion and battle.

The goal was to gain complete control of the Normandy coast. Once this was done, the troops would continue inland.

Montgomery felt confident that with all the preparations and resources they had readied, the Allies would be able to mount a successful attack and push the Germans out of France.

German Troops' Preparation

Meanwhile, Hitler, who was starting to sense that something may be coming, warned his troops that the Allies might land at Normandy even though they had believed all along the invasion would happen at Pas-de-Calais. It seemed the natural choice for a location given its proximity to Dover just across the English Channel. To prepare, three enormous gun batteries were situated on the coast of Calais by German troops. The cannons were pointed directly at Dover.

The message was clear and menacing. Calais was off-limits.

While working on the Atlantic Wall, Rommel laid out about four million mines and other traps on the beaches of Normandy, as well as in inland marshes. He also wanted the German tank divisions placed near the beaches, but German Field Marshal Karl Rudolf Gerd von Rundstedt disagreed and felt the tank divisions should be kept as a reserve. Hitler had the final say in the dispute and settled it by splitting the divisions between the three of them.

Mismanagement and disputes were not Hitler's only problems. The Allies had come up with a brilliant campaign of deception by creating a "dummy army," and Hitler fell for it completely. The campaign was given the codename Operation Fortitude, and its entire purpose was to make Hitler and the Nazis believe the Allied invasion would take place in Calais. German spy planes entailed keeping an eye on southeastern England and saw what they believed was an enormous army ready to invade. In reality, what they were looking at were mainly decoys.

England had also managed to capture almost every German spy in the country. They were either imprisoned or began working for the Allies as a double agent. The double agents were used to pass along messages to the German troops, confirming that the invasion would indeed take place in Calais.

The Allies even passed this fake message on Allied radio traffic, knowing full well that the Nazis would listen to it. When the Allies did attack, it took the German troops aback. They had not expected to be so completely wrong!

What saved the Nazis from facing total destruction immediately after the invasion was Rommel's preparation and fortification of the Atlantic Wall in Normandy. The mines, traps, and guns he had so carefully positioned gave the Germans a fighting chance and were the main reason Allied troops suffered terrible casualties.

Rommel had been adamant that Panzer tank divisions needed to be positioned and ready for an attack on the coastline, but Hitler did not agree with him. He wanted most of the Panzer divisions closely guarding Paris. The rest were scattered sporadically throughout the southern coastline. As a result, only one division was close enough to attack and defend Normandy.

Ironically, had Hitler heeded Rommel's advice and warnings, D-Day might have turned out very differently for the Allies.

Thankfully for the world, he didn't.

D-Day or the Normandy Invasion

The Normandy invasion was planned out in such a way that British, American, and Canadian forces would all land at five separate locations on the beaches of Normandy, France, at the same time.

Operation Overlord or D-Day was initially planned for May 1944, but it kept being delayed due to problems with the assembly of landing crafts, rough seas, and bad timing. It was pushed to June instead, and Eisenhower fixed June 5th as the new date for the invasion. He was adamant the date would remain firm and that there would be no more changes.

However, as June 5th approached and the Allied troops readied themselves to cross the English Channel, the weather took a turn for the worst. A violent storm swept along the French coast. The weather was so bad the Nazis were convinced they didn't need to keep watch at their posts since it would be foolhardy to brave such a stormy sea. Rommel and a few other military commanders took leave to return to Paris and Germany.

A heated debate among the Allied leaders followed, and it was decided the crossing and landing would be too dangerous under such conditions. The invasion would be delayed an additional twenty-four hours. The ships that were at sea were already brought back.

When June 5th rolled around, the Allied weather beacon indicated the weather would clear up around midnight, at least enough to go forward with the plan. The troops jumped into action.

The troops were told by Eisenhower, "You are about to embark upon the Great Crusade, toward which we have striven these many months. The eyes of the world are upon you."[6]

---

[6] Fitzgerald, Clare. "The Powerful Speech Dwight D. Eisenhower Delivered to Allied Troops Invading Normandy." https://www.warhistoryonline.com/world-war-ii/dwight-eisenhower-d-day-speech.html?chrome=1.

And indeed they were! It would be a battle that would go down in history.

In a matter of a few hours, the Allied squadron, which was made up of 2,500 ships, 3,000 landing crafts, 500 naval vessels, and other bombardment ships and escorts, began their journey from the English ports toward Normandy.

US soldiers preparing for the landing at Normandy.

*https://commons.wikimedia.org/wiki/File:Omaha_Beach_Landing_Craft_Approaches.
jpg*

Shortly after midnight, 822 aircraft—just a small fraction of the actual number of aircraft set aside for D-Day—carrying soldiers ready to land via parachutes, gliders hovering over the Normandy landing zones, and paratroopers, began landing.

Just before the landings were completed, British and American troops bombed the five beaches with the intention of destroying any gun bunkers that may have been positioned by the Germans. And by the early morning of June 6th, 1944, approximately 160,000 Allied troops had crossed the English Channel and landed on the beaches by ship and aircraft, ready to invade France. There were some casualties during the landing, as some soldiers drowned at sea or went missing, but overall, the landings were deemed a success.

The thousands of glider troops and paratroopers who had landed and were positioned behind enemy lines began working to secure roads and bridges. At 6:30 a.m., the invasions began, and Allied troops made up of British and Canadian forces were able to easily overcome the unprepared Germans and quickly capture the beaches of Sword, Gold, and Juno.

Things were not as easily managed at Utah or Omaha Beach, where things started off badly for the American troops. The force that was supposed to land on Utah ended up landing miles away because they were blown off course. But once they organized themselves, they were able to take control of Utah.

Omaha, unfortunately, faced the most challenges. The aerial bombings by the Allies didn't hit many of the targets at Omaha due to the cloudy weather, and American troops faced intense resistance from German troops. As soon as American soldiers began landing on the beach, Nazi machine guns began firing at them. More than two thousand Americans died or were wounded by the Nazis at Omaha.

By the time night fell, some 156,000 Allied troops were left. The beaches of Normandy had been stormed and were taken over with great success. Within a week, by June 11th, over 326,000 troops had swarmed the beaches and secured them completely. Meanwhile, 50,000 vehicles and over 100,000 tons of equipment arrived on the beaches.

The surprised Germans, who had been taken aback by the location of the attack, continued to deal with confusion and mismanagement. They were without the guidance of Rommel, who was on leave, while Hitler was fast asleep on the morning of the attack, having left strict instructions that he was *not* to be woken up. When he did finally wake up just before noon to absolute chaos, he refused to immediately release divisions positioned nearby for a counterattack. He was convinced the landings in Normandy were nothing more than a diversion tactic designed to shift focus from the real place of attack near the Seine River. He wanted his troops in place for that invasion.

The hugely successful Allied air campaign proved to be another sore point for the Germans. The destruction of the bridges forced the Nazis to take detours, which was time-consuming and inefficient. Allied navy troops also played a critical role in providing support and protection for the advancing ground troops.

Over the coming weeks, the Allied troops continued their advance into the Normandy countryside, undeterred by German resistance. Within weeks, the port of Cherbourg was seized successfully by the Allies and used to land nearly one million men and 150,000 vehicles. The British forces, in the meantime, gained control of Caen.

Two months later, toward the end of August 1944, Allied troops reached the Seine River. By this time, Nazi troops had been ousted from northwestern France. Paris was liberated at last. The Battle of Normandy was over.

The simple plan that had been written on one sheet of paper had been a huge success. One major goal of the Allied war effort had been achieved.

The war was not yet over, but Paris was free. The tide was definitely turning against Hitler and the Nazis. With his troops out of France, he was unable to fortify the Eastern front against the Soviet troops. This was an extremely low point for the Nazis, and things were only going to get worse.

For the Allies, however, winning the Battle of Normandy provided a much-needed boost to their morale. Although they had been winning smaller battles, this was one of the first major victories that truly signaled the end of the war. The end of the Nazi regime was near.

The estimated casualties from the Battle of Normandy are as follows:

- Germany
  - 30,000 killed
  - 80,000 wounded
  - 210,000 missing
- United States
  - 29,000 killed
  - 106,000 wounded and missing

- United Kingdom
  - 11,000 killed
  - 54,000 wounded and missing
- Canada
  - 5,000 killed
  - 13,000 wounded and missing
- France
  - 12,000 civilians killed and missing

Battle of the Bulge (December 16th, 1944– January 25th, 1945)

Hitler's Strategy

The last major battle against Hitler took place in the Ardennes region when German forces sprang a surprise attack against the Allies who were stationed in the forest in southeastern Belgium, close to Luxembourg.

The Battle of the Bulge or Battle of the Ardennes would be Hitler's last-ditch effort to win the war and Germany's last major offensive against the Allies. Hitler's goal was to split the focus of the Allies who were advancing into Germany.

After liberating Paris, Allied forces continued to travel across northern France toward Belgium, which had been occupied by the Nazis since May 1940. Soon after the invasion of Normandy, the momentum for the Allies was at a high, but as the months passed, the momentum dwindled.

In mid-November, the Allied forces launched an offensive on the Western Front, which yielded little success. The troops were exhausted, the battles were long, and no major victories were secured in the months since the liberation of France.

Hitler, in the meantime, was working hard to strengthen his troops by bringing new reserves from where he could. He was preparing to launch a new offensive. The location he chose was the woodsy, forested region of the Ardennes.

He calculated that the Allies would not expect an attack there since the terrain was difficult to work in. Hitler also liked the region because the dense woods provided the perfect shelter to conceal his forces. In addition, he timed the attack for December, deciding to use the weather as a weapon. He was banking on winter storms, blizzards, freezing rain, and cold weather to further hamper American efforts.

In Hitler's ideal world, the surprise offensive would be launched through the Ardennes, with the final aim being the crossing of the River Meuse, allowing them to recapture Antwerp, Belgium.

Along the way, the Germans would force the British Army to split from the American forces and all their supplies. In this weakened position, the German Army would swoop in to destroy the defenseless British.

Field Marshal Gerd von Rundstedt was put in charge of commanding the offensive. While this was happening, the plan was for the Fifth Panzer Army to attack the US forces in the Ardennes. The Sixth Panzer Army would move northwestward to create a strategic barrier. Hitler was well aware and wary of the Allies' superior air power, so he decided to only launch the attacks when the weather was guaranteed to keep the Allies grounded.

When the Germans began their offensive early on the morning of December 16th, 1944, in their traditional blitzkrieg style from the beginning of the war, the Allies were taken by surprise and left scrambling to mount a defense.

German divisions swept out through the dense woods of the Ardennes to attack battle-weary American troops who were stationed across a stretch of seventy-five miles to rest and regroup. As predicted by Hitler, for the first little while, the Allied air force could do absolutely nothing to retaliate due to heavy rain and mist.

Taking advantage of the general confusion from the Allies, the Nazis moved quickly and made great strides. As the Germans pressed on into the Ardennes, spilling out and around the forested area, they created a sort of "bulge" on the map. That's how the term "Battle of the Bulge" came to be.

Chaos soon descended into the Ardennes. It looked like a tornado had swept through it. Both armies blasted, hacked, and dug through the forest. As Hitler had hoped, the cold weather did not help. Over fifteen thousand American troops got sick or died just from the weather alone, suffering from pneumonia, frostbite, and trench foot.

The Nazis perhaps took notes from the deception tactics used by the Allies during the Battle of Normandy, as they attempted to deceive the Allies by sending imposters to infiltrate the troops. Road signs were changed to deliberately divert Allied troops, while German soldiers who spoke English were dressed up in American uniforms and placed in strategic locations to cause further confusion and send the real American troops to the wrong places.

These soldiers were handpicked because of their superior English skills and were trained in American slang language, which was picked up from Americans who were imprisoned in German camps. When the Allies got wind of this, they began asking American trivia questions to anyone they suspected of being a German spy.

All in all, the early days of Hitler's last great offensive were marked by confusion, chaos, heavy losses, and fear of the Allies. Was all they had so dearly gained now lost?

Allied Response and the Meuse River

But since the Allies had come so far, they would not give up so easily at this critical stage. They carried on with grit and determination, trying to find humor where they could and facing every horrifying situation with bravery and courage.

Word soon spread of the German attack, and fear gripped the hearts of people and nations who had been quietly confident that the Allies would prevail. In Belgium, the terrified civilians replaced the Allied flags with Nazi swastikas, and a curfew was imposed in Paris again. It was a sobering moment for the world at large and the United States, which had believed that victory was already within its grasp.

In the meantime, British generals quietly moved troops around to protect the crossing at the Meuse River. This river was one of the most important rivers in Europe. The majority of the Meuse River can be navigated by ships and barges and connects France to Belgium and the Netherlands.

The Albert Canal stretches from the Meuse River all the way to Antwerp, while the Juliana Canal runs parallel to the Meuse and reaches the southern tip of the Netherlands. Back in 1940, when Germany first invaded Belgium, the troops crossed the Meuse River and were able to break into France after forcefully breaching the Meuse-Albert Canal line.

The British wanted to avoid a repetition of that at all costs.

By December 24th, the Fifth Panzer Army was just over five kilometers away from the Meuse River. But the German troops' luck was finally about to run out. The Allies had finally found their groove and were starting to fight back ferociously while the Germans were facing problems with the frigid weather and gasoline shortages.

German progress was gradually slowing down.

Siege of Bastogne (December 20th–December 27th, 1944)

But before Christmas Day and the clearing of the weather, things were starting to look very bad, especially in the small town of Bastogne. The Germans needed to capture the town as part of their push toward the Meuse River.

After a few days of intense battling between the Germans and the Allies, the German troops managed to completely surround the famous 101st Airborne Division, trapping them and others within the town. But the Americans did not allow the setback to break their spirits and instead defied their captors cheerfully.

On December 22nd, 1944, the Germans demanded that the 101st Division surrender. This was flatly refused by Brigadier General Anthony McAuliffe, the commander of the division. Instead, to help them out of the situation, Eisenhower sent more troops.

Rather poetically, on Christmas Day, the weather finally cleared up. The ground was frozen solid. The Allied air force was ready for action and began a relentless campaign of air attacks, while tanks were finally able to move.

Meanwhile, as the troops continued to hold Bastogne, they suffered many casualties and waited for reinforcements. Reinforcements finally arrived on December 26th when General George Patton's Third Army arrived at Bastogne and, in rapid order, pierced through the German line, ending the siege and saving the trapped American troops.

Over the following weeks, the 101st Division and the Third Army faced off against the German forces. By January 17th, 1945, after a series of battles, the Allies had managed to push the Germans back.

End of the Battle of the Bulge

While Patton's troops were detached to Bastogne, Montgomery took the northern flank in hand. He assembled a force of whoever he could get and headed southward to stop the Germans from crossing the Meuse River.

With the Germans mere miles away from the Meuse River, the Allies successfully halted their advance. On Christmas Day, the German tanks were forced to stop and could not advance any farther toward the river. They were just six kilometers away from reaching their goal.

By this time, the Germans were nearly at the end of their rope. They had run out of supplies and were dealing with fuel and ammunition shortages. Facing resistance and pressure at every turn, on January 8th, 1945, the Germans began to slowly withdraw from the battle.

The Americans pressed on with their counteroffensive, often fighting against snow drifts and blizzards as well as the enemy. But little by little, over the coming weeks, the Allied forces' grit paid off. The German bulge shrunk, and the Allies managed to eliminate all of Germany's gains. On January 25th, 1945, the Battle of the Bulge officially ended with the Allies as the clear victors.

The Battle of the Bulge had come at a heavy price. It was the costliest battle ever fought by the American army. According to the numbers collected by the US Department of Defense, approximately 19,000 soldiers died during the battle, another 47,500 were wounded, and over 23,000 went missing. On the German side, around 100,000 soldiers were either captured, killed, or wounded.

After the battle was declared over, the Allied forces finally celebrated Christmas, doing so a month after the actual holiday. They enjoyed frozen beer shipped from the United States. But their celebration was short-lived as they now had to move on to Berlin.

End of Germany

When we consider the events in the years between 1943 and 1945, we can see a definite shift in favor of the Allies. Although Germany only officially lost in 1945 when they surrendered, some historians argue that Hitler started losing the war as early as 1941.

What went wrong with Germany's strategy and Hitler's leadership?

At first glance, Germany had it all. Better weapons. Better equipment. A better army. Better everything. The Nazis were dubbed a war machine.

But much of Germany's successes and victories in the early years were due to their blitzkrieg tactics, and their efficiency and speed fizzled out halfway through.

For all Germany's bluster and confidence, it had several weaknesses that proved fatal in the end. These included a poor economy and poor productivity during the war, fighting wars on several fronts, a lack of leadership, and weak supply lines.

Germany simply did not have the resources, such as oil, steel, and food, to launch invasions in multiple countries on such a massive scale. The country's economy did not have the prowess or production power to supply the goods the army required for their numerous invasions. And as the war wore on, these issues only got worse, and Germany's situation became increasingly desperate.

Their supply issues only started to get better in 1942 when Albert Speer, the newly appointed Minister of Armaments and War Production, began to mobilize Germany's entire economy for war. It wasn't the perfect solution, but it did start to make a difference by 1944. Unfortunately for Germany, by then, it was too late.

According to James Holland, the author of *The War in the West*, given the Nazis' supply issues, they would have needed to entirely destroy their enemies right away if they wanted to come out as winners of the war. As you know, that is not what happened. While the Germans invaded and occupied several European countries, they were unable to beat Great Britain. Hitler had arrogantly believed his Luftwaffe would easily be able to crush Britain. When this didn't happen, he was stuck fighting Britain while starting his invasion of the Soviet Union.

Holland argues that Hitler *had* to invade the Soviet Union to survive and get more resources. The invasion led to Germany overextending its resources, leaving it scrambling for supplies later.

Whether Hitler invaded the Soviet Union for survival or whether it's because that was his plan all along, the invasion did not help his or Germany's cause. When he backed out of the non-aggression pact he had signed with the Soviet Union and invaded Leningrad, he instantly made an enemy.

And not just that, by invading the Soviet Union, Hitler's troops become embroiled in a long, costly, and tedious battle on the Eastern Front, using up precious resources.

The invasion had a domino-like effect around the world. One battle led to another. Countries began to make and break pacts and agreements and look out for their own interests. Eventually, rising tensions in other parts of the world led to Japan attacking Pearl Harbor, which, as we know, would become the final straw for the United States, which had already publicly sided with Great Britain but had been reluctant to declare war.

Once the United States joined the war on the side of Great Britain, which was allied with the Soviet Union, it was a foregone conclusion that the three countries would band together to defeat their common enemy. And this was where it began to cost Hitler even more because now he was forced to divide his troops and split all his resources so that two defensive battles could be fought: one on the Western Front against the British and Americans and the other on the Eastern Front against the Soviets.

Finally, Hitler's leadership and power over the people and his troops started out strong. He ruled with an iron fist, and his followers blindly believed every word he spewed. But as the war waged, the support and faith from the German people and his own troops began to wane. There was mismanagement at every level, and many of his advisors had their own agenda.

The Battle of Normandy is a perfect example of how the lack of leadership and lack of unity among Hitler's commanders resulted in a catastrophic loss. Rommel wanted to pursue things a certain way as Germany prepared for a possible Allied invasion, but Hitler and Rundstedt disagreed with him and did not support him. On D-Day itself, while the Allied forces were landing on the beaches in Normandy, Hitler was sleeping, having left instructions that he should not be disturbed. Meanwhile, his commanders were on leave. This may have been the decisive battle that fully tipped the balance in favor of the Allies.

Even though the Allied forces had steadily begun to gain ground and win some battles, a complete victory was not within their grasp. At any moment, the war could have gone either way. The "either way" happened at the Battle of Normandy.

Another huge, decisive moment for the Allied troops was the end of the Siege of Leningrad. The Soviets' successful counteroffensive ended another long German occupation and was a huge blow to their operation. Due to the loss of France, coupled with the loss of the Soviet Union, Germany knew the end was in sight. It also knew the war would not end in their favor.

Hitler's arrogance and his refusal to admit defeat also contributed to Germany's losses. In the later years of the war, Hitler began to retreat more and more. He was seen in public very rarely and spent most of his time in his bunker in Berlin.

The other thing Germany hadn't counted on was the Allies' strength, not just in the sheer number of troops but also in resources and financial aid. A policy called the Lend-Lease Act was drafted by the United States in 1938. Under this program, the Allies were entitled to receive aid in a number of different ways. As the war went on, the program was expanded.

Through this act, Great Britain was given over thirty billion dollars of aid in supplies like weapons, aircraft, and medicine. The Soviet Union also received eleven billion dollars of aid through this program.

Because the Americans joined the war much later, the Allies had the advantage of millions of additional soldiers who were strong, healthy, and full of energy.

By the time the American troops arrived, German troops, who had been fighting non-stop for years, were tired, weak, and exhausted. It would not be surprising if they were just tired of it all.

All of these challenges and weaknesses combined proved to be too much for Germany to overcome. However, luck and fate may have also had something to do with it.

Although the war was over in Europe, the war continued on in the Pacific. Japan was a strong contender, but the Allied forces could now direct all of their attention on it. The fighting went on for another four months, but Japan eventually surrendered after the atomic bombing of Hiroshima and Nagasaki. More information on the Pacific theater can be found in Chapter 5.

Chapter 4: The Cost of War

The Second World War was one the bloodiest and deadliest military conflicts ever fought, wiping out between 3 percent and 3.7 percent of the world's entire population.

While the true numbers will never be known, historians estimate that forty to fifty million people died during the war. They died in battle, in concentration camps, and in forced labor camps. People died because of bombings, raids, famine, disease, and violence.

What was it all for? Was it worth it? The answer would likely depend on where you are currently situated in the world.

While the war was a *world* war and had a significant impact on many countries and nations, for the purpose of this book, we will examine the cost of the war for the main Allied and Axis powers. What happened to them after the war ended? What were the consequences they faced? What were the losses? The gains?

The Allied Powers

The United States

Early in the war, after Hitler began to invade countries in Europe, the United States refused to get involved. It was clear its allegiance was with the United Kingdom, but it was reluctant to formally declare war or take a position.

However, this changed when the war hit close to home. In early December 1941, Japan attacked America's naval base in Pearl

Harbor.

Casualties of War and Reparations

The US joined the war in December 1941 and fought alongside the British and the Soviets until the very end. In total, the US lost 419,000 lives. The majority of these deaths were military deaths. Very few US civilians were impacted by the war in Europe because of where the US was located. The Nazis could not subject the US to air raids as they could to the European countries. As a result, the total number of civilian deaths was around 12,100.

As part of the treaty with Germany, the United States was a recipient of reparations from the country. This will be discussed below in Germany's section.

The Post-war United States

While the loss of life cannot be viewed in a cavalier manner, in some ways, the war turned out to be a very good thing for the United States, as it reaped the most benefits.

After the First World War ended, the US went through a period of jubilance and fun called the Roaring Twenties. Money flowed freely, and the people just wanted to live and enjoy their lives.

It seemed as if things changed overnight when the stock market crashed in October 1929. The Roaring Twenties faded away, and the United States entered the Great Depression. It began in 1929 and lasted for an entire decade.

By 1939, things had started to look up, and when war broke out in Europe, it radically transformed the American economy. At that time, the country's gross national product was at \$88.6 billion; by 1944, that number had increased to \$135 billion.

How did this happen? The United States was a big country with a large population. It had the skills and available technology and money needed to increase its industrial productivity, which it did by a staggering 96 percent!

Businesses and industries began to recover, and profits began to double. After a decade of unemployment and no wages, people were working full-time again with better pay. Seventeen million jobs were created because of the war, along with new industries and technologies.

Because men were fighting in the war, women and African Americans had to take over their jobs. This would lead to social reforms and better rights for women and minorities in later years.

After the war, America's economy and global influence only got stronger. The United States had not been devastated and laid to ruin like parts of Europe. Once the war ended, the Americans had minimal rebuilding to do; instead, they focused on strengthening their industries.

Because of the role the US played during the war, the country also emerged as a global superpower.

In every way, the US came out on top after the war. By providing aid and support to the European countries ravaged by war, the US exerted a lot of influence and control over those countries, which, in turn, benefited them.

Today, the US continues to be one of the world's superpowers and is looked up to by many countries in the world as the ideal model of democracy, freedom, and rights.

Great Britain

Great Britain was on the winning side of World War II, but it had been embroiled in the war with Germany since the very beginning. British troops fought bravely and valiantly for six long years.

Although the British came out as winners, they suffered a lot of casualties and lost a great deal in the process of fighting for freedom.

Casualties of War

Great Britain lost approximately 450,900 lives during the Second World War. More than half of those deaths (383,700) were military deaths; the remaining 67,200 were civilian deaths related to military actions or activities.

Reparations

England did not have to pay any reparations and instead was the recipient of reparations from Germany as outlined in the Yalta Conference and finalized during the Potsdam Conference.

Post-war Britain

The war cost Great Britain and its colonies dearly. Even with support and aid from the United States, the war had an enormous impact on the country's economy and led to it losing the grand empire it had spent centuries building. Great Britain also lost its prestige and prominence as a global superpower, a title that was claimed by the United States.

Nazi bombing had left many parts of England in shambles and ruins. After six long years of war, the people were exhausted and mentally wrecked. The end of the war brought joy and happiness, but it also meant the start of rebuilding efforts. Reconstructing the country was a difficult task since most of Europe had to deal with shortages in goods, materials, and labor.

Great Britain's economy was a mess, and its industries were struggling. Railways and coal mines needed materials and equipment to function, but there was no money to import anything. Because the country wasn't producing much of anything, it also was not exporting anything. It seemed like a vicious, never-ending cycle.

Things were so bad that even bread had to be rationed. There seemed to be a crisis at every turn. The people faced economic and housing crises and lacked basic necessities.

But the Labour Party, under the leadership of Clement Attlee—who had been elected at the end of the war—soon established some measures, such as nationalizing the coal mines, road transport, railroads, electrical power, docks, and harbors.

Decolonization

As the war went on, it became evident to the British that holding on to their territories and colonies was becoming too costly. The colonies themselves were fueled by ideas of nationalism and wanted their independence. They no longer wanted to be ruled by the British. People from British colonies fought fearlessly alongside the British during the war and felt they deserved and had earned their freedom.

The turmoil and simmering unrest resulted in India gaining its independence from Britain in 1947. One year later, in 1948, Great Britain moved out of the Middle East. Palestine was becoming a point of contention, and the British government no longer wished to deal with it. It would go on to become an even bigger problem in later years.

What England had not considered was the loss of their African colonies. They had banked on using Africa's wealth to help rebuild England and bring back its affluence. This meant they would need to increase British presence in the continent.

However, as is so often the case in life, things did not go as planned.

Africa

A coup led by Colonel Gamal Abdel Nasser in Egypt on July 23rd, 1952, overthrew the monarchy, and a nationalist government was put in its place. When Nasser became Egypt's president, one of the first things he did was take control of the Suez Canal and nationalize it. He believed the Suez should be owned by the Egyptians. As a result of the nationalization, Great Britain lost its shares of the canal.

Wanting to get them back and put Nasser in his place, France, Britain, and Israel hatched a plot and invaded Egypt in late 1956. They eventually regained control of the canal.

The attack angered the United States, and when the matter was taken to the United Nations, the British and French were forced to withdraw from the area. This international scolding further solidified the fact that Britain was no longer an international power. It appeared as if it no longer had international authority.

As nationalism swept through Africa, Great Britain began to find it increasingly difficult to maintain power in the continent. The continued unrest and fighting began to get costly, and the profits the British had hoped to gain didn't seem worth it. It was clear they had to withdraw.

In 1960, British prime minister Harold Macmillan visited South Africa. While speaking at Cape Town, Macmillan acknowledged that Britain understood that African countries were keen to gain their independence.

Between the late 1950s and 1975, nearly two dozen African colonies fought for and gained their independence. For Great

Britain, this and the loss of its international authority are perhaps the biggest repercussions of WWII. The war triggered calls for independence and led to a dramatic shrinking of the British Empire.

Present-day Britain

Of course, Britain did not allow these setbacks to defeat it, and within a few years, the country was making significant progress in its rebuilding efforts.

From 1945 to 1979, the British government basically went back and forth between the Labour Party and the Conservatives. The Labour Party worked hard to establish initiatives designed to create a welfare state and introduced other social reforms. When the Conservatives came into power, they focused on foreign policy and oversaw the crisis with the Suez Canal.

Over the decades, each party contributed something to help rebuild the UK. Assistance from the United States under the Marshall Plan also provided much-needed relief and helped the country deal with its economic crisis. Withdrawing from its colonies also helped.

While the United Kingdom never got back its global empire or former status, it is one of the most developed nations in the world today. It is closely allied with other democratic nations and continues to wield considerable influence socially, culturally, politically, and economically around the world.

The Soviet Union

Rather ironically, the Soviet Union, which was a powerful ally to Britain and the US during the war, ended up becoming the new global enemy almost as soon as the war ended.

However the world may feel about the Soviet Union after the world war or even today, there is no doubt that without its help, Hitler and the Nazis would have been nearly impossible to defeat. The Soviet Union played a crucial role in helping the Allied powers end the war, but unfortunately, they paid a hefty price for it.

Casualties of War and Reparations

It is estimated that the Soviet Union had the highest number of casualties during World War II. Approximately 13,950,000 lives were lost.

- 6,750,000 were military deaths;
- 4,100,000 were civilian deaths caused by military action;
- 3,100,000 were civilian deaths as a result of famine and disease.

The actual number of deaths may be much higher since the Soviet Union was not keen on sharing statistics from the war, only doing so after the end of the Cold War. Historians believe that the number of deaths in the Soviet Union could be as high as twenty-seven million! They estimate that approximately 11.4 million troops died in battle, 10 million civilians died as a result of military activity, and 8 to 9 million civilians died of starvation and illness.

Over twenty-five million Soviets became homeless, and the ratio of women to men became greatly imbalanced since so many young men died during the war. An additional fourteen million soldiers suffered injuries and were wounded through the course of the war.

In terms of reparations, under the Paris Peace Treaty (1947), the Soviet Union was a recipient of reparations and entitled to receive compensation from the Axis powers. They were owed the following:

- $100 million USD from Italy;
- $300 million USD from Finland;
- $200 million USD from Hungary;
- $300 million USD from Romania.

Germany paid its reparations by sending the Soviet Union factories (which were taken apart in Germany and then shipped to the Soviet Union), industrial products, goods, and food.

After the war, the Soviet Union kept the eastern part of Poland, making it part of the Ukrainian Soviet Socialist Republic. Moldova and the three Baltic states (Estonia, Latvia, and Lithuania) also stayed under Soviet control. The USSR also took control of the governments in Bulgaria, Czechoslovakia, East Germany, Hungary, Albania, Yugoslavia, and Romania.

The Post-war Soviet Union

Within a year of the war ending, famine, epidemics, and illnesses spread through the country, lasting until 1947. On top of this, the people were struggling with drought and the repercussions of the war. The civilians suffered a lot, and it must have felt like a never-ending battle for them.

However, the exceedingly resilient population did not give up. Joseph Stalin's first priority for the Soviet Union was to rebuild. He accepted some credits from Great Britain but refused any other financial assistance, especially from the United States. Instead, they turned to the countries in Eastern Europe they were occupying for raw materials and machinery.

Emphasis was placed on modernizing their industries and arms production. By 1949, the Soviet Union had even created and successfully tested its first nuclear weapon. The German factories and supplies they received as reparations went a long way toward helping them achieve their goals.

Once the Soviet Union was able to stand on its feet, it expanded the economy and strengthened its control over Eastern Europe. In the meantime, greater control and influence were also being exerted on the population.

Under Stalin's reign, the country quickly overcame its struggles and emerged as a powerful military and industrial superpower with the goal of expanding its influence around the world. The British had ruled the world for a long time, but the war had left Great Britain weak, and its global influence had diminished significantly.

The United States, on the other hand, had come out of the war as the new superpower. Within a few years, the Soviet Union would join ranks with the US as another global superpower.

The two countries, which never had a great relationship to begin with, would go on to frequently butt heads, giving rise to an entirely new conflict.

If we consider the matter objectively, World War II helped the Soviet Union become a powerful force. Although the country suffered the most casualties and its civilian population suffered greatly from the war, the steps the government took after the war helped to establish the nation as a global power. Regardless of how many feel about the Soviet Union's politics, views, or beliefs, it has to be acknowledged that for a country that suffered such great losses, it did a remarkable job of picking up the pieces of devastation and becoming a country that nobody wanted to mess with.

It is unfortunate that, in the process, its tenuous friendship with the West came to an end, turning them from allies to foes.

The Axis Powers

Germany

Consequences of the War

Days before Germany surrendered to the Allies, Hitler shot himself and died by suicide on April 30th, 1945. Everyone who was left behind had to pick up the pieces of the carnage he instigated.

Much like the Allied powers did after World War I, Germany was punished severely for instigating World War II. In addition to suffering a humiliating defeat for the second time in less than a century, Germany also suffered enormous casualties. The country was devastated by war *and* had to pay a lot in reparations.

Basically, after nearly six years of fighting endless battles, Germany lost everything and gained nothing in return.

Casualties of War

It is difficult to have an exact number of German casualties because the numbers provided by the German High Command don't go past January 31st, 1945. However, several major battles took place after this date.

The official numbers that have been used by historians state that approximately four million German soldiers either died or went missing. However, in the 1990s, Rüdiger Overmans, a German historian, challenged this number after he dug into the military records. He conducted a study sponsored by the Gerda Henkel Foundation and discovered that the total number of dead German troops was closer to around 5.3 million. Nearly one million of them were men conscripted from countries in east-central Europe and Austria.

The final number for civilian deaths is also debated, with some believing that the number of people who died as a result of forced labor and war crimes by the Soviets and their expulsion by the Germans ranges from half a million to over two million.

It is estimated that between 350,000 to 500,000 civilians died as a result of air raids and Allied bombings. An additional 300,000 people died in Germany as a result of religious persecution, racism, and politics.

And finally, approximately 200,000 German people who suffered from disabilities were killed as part of the Nazis' euthanasia programs.

The Yalta Conference

The question of what should be done about Germany was a point of discussion for the Allied powers months before the war actually ended. When they met in February 1945 in a city called Yalta, along the coast of the Crimean Peninsula, they were confident the war was already won.

The meeting of the three major Allied leaders—US President Roosevelt, British Prime Minister Churchill, and Soviet Premier Stalin—was aptly titled the Yalta Conference.

Churchill, Roosevelt, and Stalin (left to right) at Yalta.

https://commons.wikimedia.org/wiki/File:Yalta_Conference_1945_Churchill,_Stalin,_Roosevelt.jpg

When the three powers had met previously in November of 1943 in Tehran, they had discussed strategies on how to liberate Paris and defeat Germany. By the time of the Yalta meeting, Paris had been liberated, and Germany was on the verge of being crushed.

Now, they needed to figure out what to do about Japan, which was still going strong at that time. Roosevelt was certain that without a clear strategy, the war in the Pacific would continue. He wanted to make sure the Soviet Union would support the US, and he also wanted them to join the United Nations.

Churchill wanted to discuss how to bring about democracy in Eastern and Central Europe. Stalin was plotting how best to expand the Soviet Union's influence.

After much discussion, some key points were agreed upon.

- Germany would have to surrender unconditionally, and the country would be divided into four zones to be occupied by the four Allied powers.

- All of Germany, including civilians and prisoners of war, would be punished severely for what they had done. This would be done via reparations.

- Poland would be allowed free elections.

- The Soviet Union would take a seat in the UN Security Council as a permanent member and would go to war against Japan once Germany was dealt with.

The leaders left the conference feeling confident about their next steps. However, it would soon become apparent that Stalin wouldn't do what he said he would.

Another meeting was held between July 17th and August 2nd, 1945, called the Potsdam Conference. This conference would decide Germany's post-war fate.

The Potsdam Conference

At one point, Germany was on an unstoppable high. Nazi troops were stealing from countries, demanding forced labor, and taking whatever they wanted with little care about the destruction they were leaving behind. The end of the war was a sobering moment for Germans, especially when it came time to discuss how they would repay the damage, chaos, and catastrophe they had caused around the world.

Since the initial discussion in Yalta couldn't be relied upon, a new conference was organized. In the five months since the Yalta Conference had taken place, some major changes in personnel had happened. Roosevelt had died just three months earlier, so President Harry Truman attended the conference. Churchill came, but he lost an election halfway through the conference and was replaced by Clement Attlee, the new prime minister. On the Soviet side, nothing had changed, and Stalin was in attendance.

During the Potsdam Conference, the Allies decided Germany would pay $23 billion USD, the bulk of which would be paid with factories and machinery. We will discuss some of the key highlights of the conference below.

Annexation

It was agreed that all the countries that had been annexed by the Nazis would be returned to their pre-war borders, including Hungary, Czechoslovakia, and western Poland.

Occupation

Austria and Germany were divided into four zones that would be occupied and controlled by four of the Allied powers: Great Britain, France, the Soviet Union, and the United States.

All costs and expenses incurred by the occupying countries would need to be paid for by Germany. By the time the occupation of the four zones ended in 1950, these expenses had amounted to several billion dollars.

The German Military

The treaty demanded the demilitarization of Germany, as well as its democratization and denazification.

Industries and Rail Infrastructure

When the four Allied powers began to occupy the four zones, whatever was left of German industries was dismantled. Factories, plants, railroad systems, machinery...everything.

After taking them apart, they were taken to Allied countries. Germany's ships and merchant fleet were also taken. Whatever industries were left and still producing had to give a share to the

Allies. Industrial productions, including steel and coal, were all taken out of the country as well.

Germany had foreign stocks that had a value of approximately 2.5 billion dollars. This, too, was confiscated.

Double track railways in the zone occupied by the Soviet Union were dismantled and turned into one track. The Soviet Union took away the rest of the materials.

In short, Germany was stripped bare of every salvageable good and material. Almost everything of value was taken away. However, after a few years of doing this, the Allied powers, with the exception of the Soviet Union, backed off a little and implemented the Marshall Plan. The Soviet Union, however, continued to take goods and materials from Germany until 1953.

Victims of the Holocaust

Germany agreed to provide compensation to the Holocaust victims. The treaty also outlined the intent to prosecute Nazi war criminals and hold them accountable for their actions during the war, especially in concentration camps. (More details about the Holocaust and the atrocities the Nazis perpetrated will be talked about in Chapter 9.)

Other Terms

Germany was in possession of around ten billion dollars' worth of intellectual property. These were in the form of trademarks, copyrights, patents, and other things. Like the stocks, this was taken away by the Allies.

Another condition in the treaty demanded that Germany provide forced labor to the Allies for a number of years. The laborers would be required to work in mines or industries or on farms or camps.

Reparations from Germany

In addition to the conditions outlined in the Potsdam Conference, Germany had to pay reparations to several countries that had been left in shambles due to either Nazi aggression or occupation.

Poland

In 1953, pressured by the Soviet Union, the People's Republic of Poland waived any reparations from Germany. In exchange for waiving this right, Poland and Russia wanted Germany to accept the Oder-Neisse border. Accepting this border meant that Germany would have to give up a quarter of its borders to the two countries.

In 1990, after German reunification, Poland asked for reparations. The Foundation for Polish-German Reconciliation was established in 1992, and around 4.7 billion zlotys were paid to the Polish people by Germany. Compensation continued to be paid by Austria and Germany to surviving Polish victims until 2006.

Even today, it is still widely debated whether Germany actually owes Poland any reparations or not, given the Polish had waived that right in 1954.

Greece

The Nazi occupation of Greece resulted in enormous losses and the destruction of the country. Greece was even forced to take out large sums of money from its banks and hand them over to Nazi Germany as a "loan."

Under the Paris Reparation Treaty, Greece received a share of the reparations taken by the Allies. When the Paris Peace Treaties were finalized in 1947, Greece was awarded an additional share of reparations.

In 1960, 115 million German marks were given as compensation to Greek people who had been victims of the Nazis. The Greek government later demanded more money and claimed the payment before was simply one of many payments to come.

A final treaty was signed in 1990 between Britain, France, the US, the Soviet Union, and East and West Germany. It was called the Treaty on the Final Settlement with Respect to Germany, and it put an end to any and all questions about Germany after the war. Based on this treaty, Germany considers all questions regarding reparations to be resolved.

Greece did not agree. In 2015, it began to call on Germany to pay the reparations still owed to them. The current balance of the reparations, according to Greece's calculations, stands at 279 billion euros.

Israel

Reparations for Jewish property confiscated by Germany and the Nazis were made to Israel by West Germany. Payments totaling approximately $14 billion USD were made until 1989.

The Netherlands

Initially, the Netherlands asked Germany to pay them twenty-five billion guilders. This demand was later changed, and they requested to annex a part of Germany instead. In 1949, around sixty-nine square kilometers were annexed by the Netherlands.

Nearly fifteen years later, in 1963, West Germany paid the Netherlands 280 million German marks and bought the territory back.

Yugoslavia

Germany paid Yugoslavia around $36 million USD in equipment and material taken from their factories. An additional eight million German marks were paid to Yugoslav citizens as compensation for forced experimentation.

The Soviet Union

The Soviet Union received reparations from Germany through machines, factories, industrial production, raw materials, food, and other supplies. The Memel Territory from Lithuania, which was annexed by Germany prior to the start of the war, was annexed by the Soviets after the end of the war.

To this day, many of the reparations have not been paid in full to the recipient countries, and it is unlikely that they ever will be. Most countries have moved on from their desire to punish Germany and demand payback. However, the question of reparations occasionally rears its head, but whether anything will come of these requests remain to be seen.

Post-war Germany

After Germany collapsed and surrendered to the Allies, one of the treaty's conditions was that the Allied powers would occupy the country.

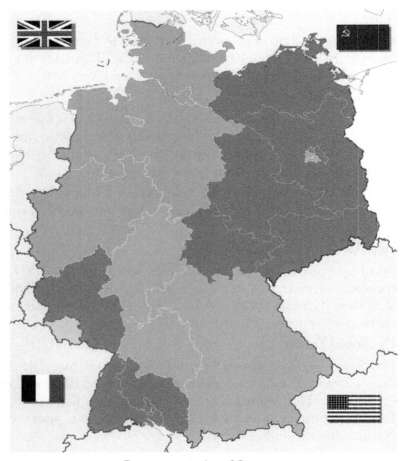

Post-war occupation of Germany.

WikiNight2, GFDL <http://www.gnu.org/copyleft/fdl.htm >, via Wikimedia Commons; https://commons.wikimedia.org/wiki/File:Deutschland_Besatzungszonen_8_Jun_1947_-_22_Apr_1949.svg

The country was divided by the four powers in the following fashion:

- Great Britain took over the northwest part of the country.
- France was put in control of the southwest portion.
- The United States had its zone in the south.
- The Soviet Union got the east.

84

In addition to this division, territories that fell to the east of the Oder and Neisse Rivers were shifted under the Polish. This led to a great displacement; nearly fifteen million people of German ethnicity were made to leave the area. The expulsion was not a seamless and successful process and resulted in a huge number of civilian deaths. People froze, became ill, starved, were abused, or were forced to work in labor camps.

By 1949, West Germany organized itself and established the Federal Republic of Germany. This was occupied by the UK, France, and the US. In the meantime, East Germany, which was occupied by the Soviet Union, established the German Democratic Republic.

East and West Germany would go on to have very different futures. The divide was both physical and ideological, with two differing beliefs. West Germany followed a Westernized model of government, while East Germany was subjected to communist rule.

What's interesting is that Berlin was also divided between the four occupiers. This would become hugely significant in less than two decades when the Berlin Wall went up, resulting in a physical barrier separating the two ideologies and two different ways of life.

West Germany

When the rubble from the war was cleared, it unveiled a striking truth: Germany, for all its victories and triumphs, had been left decimated and crippled. Large portions of the country were in utter ruins. And since Germany faced harsh reparations, its prospects for the future did not look promising.

Therefore, it was shocking and unexpected when within four decades, the country emerged as not just *a* global economic power but one with the third-largest global economy. This is often referred to as the *Wirtschaftswunder* or "economic miracle."

How did Germany do it?

Significant credit is owed to the internationally renowned economist Walter Eucken. He fought during the First World War and eventually became a professor at the University of Freiburg. While teaching, he began to develop economic theories. These theories were rooted in the concept of free-market capitalism with input from the government to prevent monopolies by any one company or group of people. He also believed the government would consider the interests of all people instead of a select few.

Eucken also developed theories on a social welfare system to provide assistance to those less fortunate and promoted the idea of a central bank that was not tied to the government. He argued that a centralized financial institution would help keep the economy stable by using monetary policies.

The theories he put forward are essentially the way most Western or developed countries operate, but when they were initially proposed, they seemed like an entirely foreign concept. Emphasis was instead placed on the idea of socialism.

In the middle of the socialism vs. free-market capitalism debate, a man named Ludwig Erhard, who was mentored by Eucken, began to gain a certain reputation and caught the attention of US intelligence forces. After Germany's surrender, he became the finance minister of Bavaria. He eventually worked his way up to director of the economic council in Allied-occupied West Germany.

Under his direction, a new currency was created, reducing the amount of money available by nearly 93 percent! This resulted in a dramatic reduction of wealth for affluent Germans and companies. He also implemented large tax cuts designed to help people spend and invest their money. The new money came into effect in late June 1948. Price controls were also removed, which left Erhard's superiors questioning his decisions. But Erhard held firm, and the gamble paid off—big time.

When people realized the money had value, they began to shop again. Black market dealings ceased, and people were filled with a desire to earn gainful employment once more because they actually had an incentive to work.

This shift in mentality led to increased productivity. For example, in June 1948, the country's industrial production was half of what it had been over a decade prior in 1936. Within five to six months of the new currency being introduced, industrial production had reached nearly 80 percent! And by 1958, industrial production had quadrupled.

The Marshall Plan, which was created by George Marshall, the US Secretary of State, also helped Germany turn things around. Under the Marshall Plan, around $15 billion USD was distributed to European countries that had suffered enormous losses from the war. A large portion of this aid was given to Germany.

It was also lucky for West Germany that it was occupied by the UK, France, and the US. The influence of these powers and having America as a close ally helped the rebuilding process.

The perfect comparison can be found just on the other side of the ideological border in Soviet-controlled East Germany.

East Germany

Unlike West Germany, East Germany did not enjoy the same benefits and prosperity. Its economy continued to lag, and political freedoms diminished substantially. Things became so bad that people from East Germany became desperate to leave, willing to defy the stringent travel restrictions.

As a way of preventing East German residents from leaving, the Soviet Union began constructing a concrete barrier. The Berlin Wall went up in 1961, and it became a global symbol of the Cold War and a divided Europe.

The residents of East Germany would remain trapped on the other side of the wall until November 9th, 1989, when large crowds swarmed the wall and began to dismantle it. The wall's dismantling came about after the East German Communist Party told the people that they were allowed to cross the border if they wished. The Berlin Wall fell that day. In 1990, the two parts of Germany reunited. The following year, the USSR was officially dissolved.

Today, Germany is a democratic developed nation. It is considered to be a superpower and is one of the most technologically advanced countries. It has a strong military and has one of the largest trading blocs in the world. It is also part of the European Union.

Germany put the events of WWII behind them while still remembering the destruction it had caused. The nation is a strong ally in the West and is focused on maintaining global peace and stability. The country belongs to both the North Atlantic Treaty Organization (NATO) and the United Nations (UN).

Italy

Consequences of the War

Italy paid a steep price for its role in the war. They got almost nothing out of it, and until their surrender in 1943, the war was just a series of military disasters for the country.

Casualties of War and Reparations

Not only did Italy lose its empire in East Africa, but it also lost approximately 492,400 to 514,000 troops in battle. A further 150,000 civilians are estimated to have died during the war.

Under the terms of the 1947 Treaty of Peace with Italy, Italy had to pay reparations to several countries.

- $125 million USD to Yugoslavia
- $105 million USD to Greece
- $100 million USD to the Soviet Union
- $25 million USD to Ethiopia
- $5 million USD to Albania

Under the treaty, Italy had to give up all its African colonies. Some of its Alpine territories went to France, while the Dodecanese, a group of Greek islands, was given to Greece.

During the war, many factories in northern Italy were completely destroyed due to Allied bombing. Production capacities in these factories dropped dramatically, leaving them unable to produce any weapons or other items.

Italians around the world also faced repercussions. Italian immigrants living in Great Britain and the United States were automatically assumed to have fascist ties or beliefs. Thousands of immigrants found themselves rounded up and displaced. They lost their citizenship and their properties and were treated like the enemy even if they were not.

By the time Italy had surrendered to the Allies, the country was in utter shambles. They had lost their empire in Africa, their cities had been destroyed, they were barely producing anything, and they couldn't see a way out of the mess. Surrender seemed like the best and only option available to them.

Within days of Mussolini's arrest, the Fascist Party and other fascist institutions dissolved. The interim government that was put in place was made up almost entirely of ex-fascists. Soon after, Italy broke ties with Germany, ending their alliance. Germany invaded Rome almost immediately. Within months, in a complete reversal from the start of the war, Italy had declared war on Germany. Now it was the Allies helping them out!

Post-war Italy

When the war finally came to an end in May 1945, a strong anti-fascist movement spread over the country. Before the end of the war, in 1943, all the political parties that were strongly opposed to fascism had joined together to form a political umbrella organization called the National Liberation Committee (*Comitato di Liberazione Nazionale* or CLN). The CLN began a resistance movement against the Nazis and was backed by the Allied powers and Italy's monarchy.

Once the war ended, Ferruccio Parri, the leader of the political party Party of Action, led the government.

Throughout Italy, thousands of fascists were found and killed, and a special committee was even set up to purge the country of fascists. This caused significant concern amongst the population, especially among people who held positions in the public sector. A backlash followed, and Ferruccio soon resigned. A more moderate and democratic leader named Alcide De Gasperi replaced him. He stopped the purges and brought order to the country.

One year after the end of the war, King Victor Emmanuel III abdicated in favor of his son, King Umberto II. He didn't hold the position for too long. The country held a referendum and decided they no longer wanted a monarchy and wanted to become a republic. The entire royal family was forced to leave Italy.

When the Cold War began in 1947, De Gasperi went to the United States. In order to keep the Vatican and the United States happy, he had made sure to exclude communists and socialists from his government. His visit to the US proved very fruitful, as he returned with $150 million USD in aid. It was understood that if any communists came to power, the aid would be revoked.

Italy was left off in a better situation post-World War II. The country became a republic and more democratic. Italy developed closer ties with the United States, relying on them for much-needed financial aid. Joining the war effort on the side of the Allies also put Italy on the "right side" of history. Joining the North Atlantic Treaty Organization (NATO) also went a long way to solidifying its position as a Western ally.

In the years after the war, with the help of the US, Italy was able to rebuild many industries and see economic growth. Its currency stabilized, and it joined the European trade, becoming known for its luxurious brand names and fashionable clothing.

Over time, Mussolini and his fascist regime became a thing of the past and are seen as a bump in the road to Italy's long and colorful history.

Japan

The consequences and losses for Japan post-WWII were catastrophic.

During the war, Japan was one of the main enemies of the Allies and paid for it dearly. The atomic bombs dropped on Hiroshima and Nagasaki brought utter devastation to the country. Their effects would last for decades to come.

Japan lost lives, money, and infrastructure. It would take years to reconstruct parts of the country that had been destroyed by atomic bombs and countless air raids.

Casualties of War and Reparations

Japan lost over 3,100,000 people in the war. Approximately 2,300,000 soldiers and troops died, while the remaining 800,000 deaths were civilians. These numbers don't take into account the thousands of people who died in the years since due to the long-term effects of the atomic bombs. Many civilians who survived the bombings would go on to become sick from cancer, leukemia, or other health issues related to radiation.

Japan paid dearly financially as well. Based on the Treaty of Peace with Japan (1951), which was signed by forty-nine nations, it was agreed that the Allied powers would receive reparations from Japan for the damage the country inflicted.

In total, fifty-four bilateral agreements were included in the treaty. Some of the reparations requested include:

- $550 million USD to the Philippines

- $39 million USD to South Vietnam

- $4.5 million sterling pounds to the International Committee of the Red Cross in order to provide compensation to prisoners of war

- $20 million USD to Burma

- $300 million USD to South Korea

- $223.8 million USD to Indonesia

- $5.5 million USD to Spain

Japan started paying these reparations in 1955. The payments ended in 1977. The complete document outlining all the reparations can be found in the Treaty of Peace with Japan.[7]

Occupation of Japan

While the Japanese surrender officially brought the Second World War to an end, it wasn't really the end. The question of what to do with Japan was discussed at great length during a number of conferences held between the Allied leaders. There were questions about Japan's army, its colonies, its economy, etc.

Soon after the war ended, the US led a mission of Allied forces to occupy and rehabilitate Japan. For eight years, they occupied the country under the direction of General Douglas MacArthur, who was the Supreme Commander for the Allied Powers (SCAP). The United Kingdom, China, and the Soviet Union were also involved in the rebuilding plans as advisors.

Sweeping and dramatic changes were brought into the country in three phases. The bulk of the changes took place in the first phase, which roughly lasted from 1945 to 1947. Japan's government was completely dismantled, and military officers were forbidden from any kind of leadership or political role in the new government. War crime trials were held in Tokyo.

---

[7] https://treaties.un.org/doc/publication/unts/volume%20136/volume-136-i-1832-english.pdf

The empire was gone. While the emperor of Japan was kept on as a figurehead, he had no political power or control. The government was overhauled and replaced by a democracy, and a parliamentary system was established.

Land reforms were introduced, which significantly reduced the amount of power and influence wielded by wealthy landowners. MacArthur also made it his mission to convert Japan's economy into a free market. Rights, privileges, and equality for women were also promoted.

The second phase between 1947 and 1950 was characterized by an economic crisis and growing concerns about communist ideologies spreading through the country. MacArthur felt strongly that a weak economy would make Japan and its population more vulnerable to communist tendencies. With China already headed down the path of communism, the Allied forces realized they had to change course.

Fixing the economy became a priority. Tax reforms were introduced, but the war in North Korea became Japan's saving grace. When the United Nations joined the war, Japan supplied everything the UN forces needed. This also helped secure Japan's position and safety on the world map.

In 1950, the third and final phase began. Five years into the occupation, the Allied forces were starting to feel confident that they had laid out a solid foundation for Japan's economic and political success.

The process of drafting a formal treaty that would officially end the war and the occupation began. Faced with the threat of communism and the Soviet Union, the idea of Japan having an army no longer made the United States nervous, nor did they see the country as a threat any longer.

In the final treaty, the two countries signed a bilateral security pact, although the US base in Okinawa was allowed to remain. The occupation officially ended in 1952.

Post-occupation Japan

All things considered, Japan came out stronger at the end of the war and occupation. In many ways, the occupation by the Allied forces was the best thing that could have happened to the country. Instead of being left to deal with their post-war mess on their own, the US helped to rebuild the country into a much stronger one. The country became democratic, and women were given privileges, such as the right to vote, something they did have before.

Today, Japan is a very prosperous country. It is one of the most developed and most educated countries in the world and has a fairly wealthy population. The country boasts low unemployment rates and has the second-largest economy in the world.

Today, the US and Japan share a very close relationship; their former enmity is a thing of the past. They are allies, friends, and great supporters of one another. To many, the US occupation of Japan can be considered a success story.

Part Two: Theaters of War

Chapter 5: The War at Sea

Battles on land, such as the Battle of Normandy or the Battle of the Bulge, are often talked about and written about when discussing the Second World War. While land wars made up the majority of the battles, naval warfare played a crucial role in how the war unfolded and the direction it went in.

In this chapter, we will look at a few significant battles that took place at sea and discuss what the repercussions of these battles were and how they contributed to the war effort.

Battle of the Atlantic (1939–1945)

The Battle of the Atlantic started at the beginning of the Second World War. It played out on the Atlantic Ocean, where German submarines launched a campaign of viciously attacking ships and convoys that were carrying supplies to the Allied forces.

The Battle of the Atlantic started in 1939 and was a continuous battle that lasted for the entire duration of the war. It ended in 1945, making it the longest battle of the war. The battle resulted in over seventy thousand deaths on the Allied side. The Germans lost about thirty thousand people.

It officially began on September 3rd, 1939, several hours after Great Britain declared war on Germany. The SS *Athenia* was headed to Montreal with over 1,400 passengers when it was attacked and destroyed by a German submarine, leading to the deaths of 112 people.

With the attack on the SS *Athenia*, the war on the sea had begun, with Germany fighting for control of the shipping routes through the Atlantic Ocean. The Germans believed that destroying ships carrying critical supplies like food, equipment, and oil would cripple the Allied forces and leave them in a weaker position.

Days later, on September 10th, Canada, a former colony and close ally of Great Britain, declared war on Germany as well. Canada is credited with playing a key role in the battle. Overnight, the Canadian Armed Forces were given the responsibility of escorting convoys to Europe. The convoys were also protected by the Royal Air Force (RAF). Through the course of the battle, the RAF sank nineteen German U-boats, while the RAF Coastal Command sank about two hundred U-boats.

At the beginning of the war, the Nazis were tasting victory after victory in their battles on land. A similar type of success was being seen at sea.

German Admiral Karl Dönitz was the man in charge of leading the naval side of the war, and he put in place a highly successful and extremely deadly strategy. The Allied convoys were hunted and cornered in groups; it was as if the Nazis were acting like a wolf pack. Dönitz assigned groups of submarines to cover a certain area on the route. As soon as a convoy was visible, the message was passed along to the other U-boats nearby, and they all gathered together. Under cover of darkness, the "wolf pack" would strike the convoy simultaneously.

Dönitz's strategy was first used on October 18th, 1940, when a total of seven German submarines attacked a convoy heading for England. A battle ensued, lasting for three days. The German submarines sank 20 of the 35 merchant ships, killing 140 sailors.

The Black Pit

A specific stretch of the Atlantic Ocean that fell beyond the aerial coverage of the Allies was called the Black Pit. The Black Pit would become the scene of many naval battles and attacks.

The German commanders gained confidence from the success of their attacks and decided to go a little further by sending U-boats along the coast of the United States and Canada. The U-boats destroyed the oil tankers and ships headed toward Nova Scotia, where they would have formed part of a convoy that would then go to Europe.

By May 1942, the U-boats were on the St. Lawrence River, sinking a total of twenty-one ships, including a ferry. For six months, from March to September, German U-boats were sinking roughly one hundred ships a month! By this point, around two thousand merchant ships had been destroyed by the Germans, killing several thousand sailors in the process. Millions of tons of supplies headed for the Allied forces fighting in Europe never reached them and were sunk instead.

The Turning Tide

Again, like the battles on land, the tide also turned for those battling at sea.

The British were able to crack the Germans' secret code, which went a long way toward helping the Allies. They were no longer flying blind and were able to have a better idea of what the Germans would do next.

Cracking the Enigma code also allowed the Allies to monitor the movements of U-boats. In addition to this, due to the development of long-range aircraft, the Allies were able to cover more ground (or rather water) when it came to the Atlantic.

The British navy took a more aggressive approach toward the German U-boats and actively began to track them down. They were also on the constant lookout for convoys that needed immediate assistance.

Additional support and assistance arrived from Canada in the form of ships. Canada's navy also began to hunt German U-boats and helped sink additional boats. This mighty combination began to pay off, and the tide began to turn.

In 1942, the Germans were sinking an average of one hundred merchant ships a month; in 1943, they managed to sink less than three hundred ships throughout the year! When the Germans began to suffer huge losses and lose their own U-boats at an alarming rate, they pulled back for a few months.

Canada's support resulted in all of the northwestern Atlantic falling under its command. It was up to Canada to keep the

Germans in line at sea.

Although the Germans were struggling, they were not ready to give up just yet and still had a few more cards to play. Five years into the war, technology had greatly improved. The Germans now had much better submarines and were getting increasingly desperate, which meant Allied convoys on the Atlantic were still in danger.

Toward the end of the war, the Germans torpedoed the HMCS *Esquimalt* near Halifax, Canada. Forty-four people died. Three weeks after the attack, the U-boat that had carried out the attack, *U-190*, finally surrendered, bringing the battle to an end.

Although the Battle of the Atlantic is not discussed exhaustively, it played a critical role, as it helped the Allied forces that were fighting in Europe. The naval forces kept the sea safe, allowing for the passage of precious goods and supplies to Europe and contributing hugely to the Allies' eventual victory.

The long, drawn-out battle was draining and relentless and claimed the lives of over seventy thousand merchant seamen. Most of whom never made it back home. Their bodies were never recovered as they sank into the Atlantic Ocean.

Black Sea Campaigns (1941–1944)

The Black Sea campaigns took place in the Black Sea and its surrounding coastal regions. It was fought by the Axis powers and the Soviet Union between 1941 to 1944.

The Soviet Navy, called the Black Sea Fleet, was completely taken aback when Hitler broke his non-aggression pact with Stalin and invaded the country.

The Axis forces in the Black Sea campaigns were made up of Germans, Italians, Bulgarians, and Romanians. The Croatian Naval Legion also joined after it was established in July 1941.

The Soviet Navy was far superior to what the Axis had to offer. However, things started badly for them because not only had they been unprepared for the attack, but Germany's Luftwaffe was also very efficient and powerful. A series of bombings destroyed most of the Soviet ships.

Hitler's invasion of the Soviet Union, codenamed Operation Barbarossa, began on June 22nd, 1941. The Soviet Union suffered devastating losses on every front, but they were beginning to resist and fight back.

On August 8th, the Germans besieged the port of Odesa, which is located on the Black Sea. A battle ensued between the Axis and the Soviet forces, lasting for seventy-three days. By mid-October, the Black Sea Fleet decided to evacuate the garrison to the city of Sevastopol. It also evacuated nearly 350,000 civilians and military personnel.

During the start of Sevastopol's invasion, the Black Sea Fleet did everything in its power to defend the city. Soviet submarines sank thousands of tons of Axis supplies, while the southern Black Sea was scattered with minefields placed there by both the Axis and the Soviet Union. The minefields sunk several submarines on both sides.

Most of the Black Sea campaigns in 1942 were related to the Siege of Sevastopol. Supplies and other support were provided by Soviet warships during the winter and spring.

In February of 1942, while active Soviet submarines were monitoring the western part of the Black Sea, *Shch-213*, a Soviet submarine, torpedoed *Struma*, a ship that was sailing with the Red Cross flag. It was carrying around eight hundred Jewish refugees from Romania and taking them to Palestine. Everyone on board except for one person died.

By the following year, the Black Sea Fleet had been greatly reduced and was in poor condition. The Romanian Naval Forces had also suffered some losses but were performing admirably.

During 1943, most of the operations on the Black Sea were offensive campaigns launched by the Soviet Union. In July, the Soviet submarine *M-31* was sunk by a Romanian destroyer.

By this time, it was clear to the Axis that things were not going well for them as a whole, so Germany decided to evacuate the "Goth's head position," also known as Kuban Bridgehead. The bridgehead was located on the Taman Peninsula, which was situated between the Black Sea and the Sea of Azov. It was created after Germany was driven out of the Caucasus. The Germans had heavily fortified the area and had military personnel stationed there so they could start attacking the Caucasus when needed.

But when things started to go badly with the Red Army, the Germans decided to cut their losses and evacuate from the area. As they evacuated, they made sure to sink several Soviet destroyers with their Stukas (German dive bombers).

When the Second World War entered its fifth year, the Soviet fleet was almost in shambles and non-functioning. They were badly in need of repairs, and it seemed as if there was no way forward. As a result, they began to use smaller vessels in most of their offensive campaigns. The naval air force also lent its support.

But by 1944, things were looking very bad for the Axis. They were losing land battles on almost every front, with Axis troops trapped in the Crimea after Odesa's liberation. Axis forces near Sevastopol had also surrendered while Soviet submarines carried on with their attacks on Axis ships.

The Red Air Force was also playing an active role by raiding Axis bases located in the Black Sea and sinking U-boats and other targets. Their efforts reduced the number of German submarines by half!

As things continued to deteriorate for the Nazis, the Soviets gained more ground, bringing the Black Sea campaigns to an end.

Baltic Sea campaigns (1939–1945)

While the Soviets were busy fighting the Axis powers along the Black Sea, Allied forces were battling the Axis on the Baltic Sea. Although the main participants on the Allied side in this theater were the Soviet Union and the Polish Navy, the Swedish Navy also played a crucial role in the campaigns. On the Axis side, the German Navy was supported by the Finnish Navy.

The Polish Navy had first entered the picture in 1939 when the country was invaded by Germany during the Battle of Danzig Bay and the Battle of Hel.

The Battle of Danzig would be the first battle of WWII involving both naval forces and air forces. While the Polish flotilla was sailing across Danzig Bay, they were attacked by the Luftwaffe. The Polish warships managed to avoid most of them, suffering some damage. When they finally arrived at Hel, they were met with additional air raids on September 1ˢᵗ, 1939.

Within days, the Luftwaffe had severely damaged or destroyed the Polish ships, which were either abandoned or sank. The few remaining light vessels, such as tugboats and gunboats, that had survived were taken by the Germans.

In 1941, the Soviet Red Banner Baltic Fleet was in a good position. It had the Baltic Sea's largest navy with bases scattered all along the coast. But when Germany invaded suddenly and with no warning, the unprepared Soviet fleet began to evacuate frantically from Finland and the Baltic states.

In the process, they lost their naval bases at Liepaja and Riga, as well as a significant part of their navy. They took refuge in Tallinn, but it didn't remain a refuge for long since they were soon surrounded by German troops.

The Soviets were now scrambling to evacuate everyone from the sea while being attacked relentlessly by German bombers. During the evacuation, the Soviets suffered heavy losses at the Juminda Peninsula, which had been packed with mines by the Germans and Finnish.

A similar story unfolded at Hango, another Soviet naval base. While evacuating Hango toward the end of the year, the Soviet Navy again suffered massive losses.

What the Soviet Navy had been able to do was save Leningrad from Germany's first assault back in the fall. Of course, that, too, would be short-lived, as German troops went on to blockade Leningrad.

In 1942, the Oranienbaum Bridgehead was maintained by the Soviets. They sent out submarines to attack German and Finland and were able to successfully sink eighteen ships. However, in the process, they lost twelve of their submarines.

Even though it wasn't the most successful campaign, the Soviet Navy made the Axis navies uncomfortable and forced them to use longer alternate routes. In order to get rid of the Soviet Navy, the Germans began to use more aggressive tactics, leading to increased losses for the Soviets.

In January 1942, the Soviets recaptured Suursaari from the Finnish, but within a couple of months, the Finnish managed to drive them out. This set off a series of battles that would last until

April, with both sides fighting to regain control of the island.

When the Soviets tried to capture another island, Someri, they were forced back but managed to damage two Finnish gunboats in the process.

In the fall of 1942, Finland sent out its improved and updated submarines to the Sea of Aland to search for Soviet submarines. They destroyed three Soviet submarines in total, which led to them pulling back a little from the area.

By the time spring of 1943 rolled around, the Germans were ramping up their efforts in the Black Sea. The Gulf of Finland was protected by mines, and the Soviets were unable to break through the anti-submarine net barrage across the gulf. Over sixty thousand naval mines were spread out in the area. The Soviets were prevented from raiding German shipping or from getting anywhere close to the German U-boats. Their repeated attempts came at a high cost since they lost six submarines.

However, the Soviets did sink one of the Finnish minelayers and caused damage to gunboats through an air raid. In the fall of 1943, one of the Soviet Union's torpedo planes sank a Finnish escort vessel.

By 1944, the Soviets were starting to crush the Axis powers in land battles. The Siege of Leningrad had been lifted, and things were looking up for the Allied powers.

Air raids on Helsinki by the Soviets led to the sinking of two Finnish patrol boats; however, the Soviets were unsuccessful in their attempt to attack the south coast of the Gulf of Finland. In the end, that didn't matter. In September, the Soviet Union and Finland signed the Moscow Armistice, agreeing to peace.

Prior to the armistice, the Soviet offensives against Finland resulted in several German vessels becoming damaged. After the successful invasion of Normandy, the majority of Germany's surface fleet was sent to the Baltic Sea to help the floundering navy there. A series of battles ensued between the two countries, with the Soviets advancing further into Nazi-occupied territories and the Germans evacuating people. Both sides continued with their bombings and torpedoing, resulting in boats and vessels sustaining significant damage.

By this time, the German forces were also dealing with a desperate shortage of supplies, including fuel. In order to save whatever resources they had left, the Germans began to reduce the number of escort ships, leaving the convoys open to the Soviets' mercy.

After liberating Leningrad, the Soviet Union's weakened and crumbling surface fleet stayed put because of the mines the Germans had laid out in the area. Its submarines, however, continued to attack and sank several German liners that were being used to transport refugees, resulting in heavy losses. The war ended soon after that, bringing an end to the Baltic Sea campaigns.

Pacific Theater

When people discuss WWII, Europe tends to get more attention, but Japan played a very critical role in the war. Japan, which was part of the Axis, was in conflict with much of Asia and later the United States and the Allies.

After the attack on Pearl Harbor, the United States went into the war with guns blazing. Defeating Germany was certainly a priority for the US but so was crushing Japan.

Japan's sphere of influence and control extended over a large portion of central Pacific and Southeast Asia, including Burma, present-day Malaysia, New Guinea, and Wake Island.

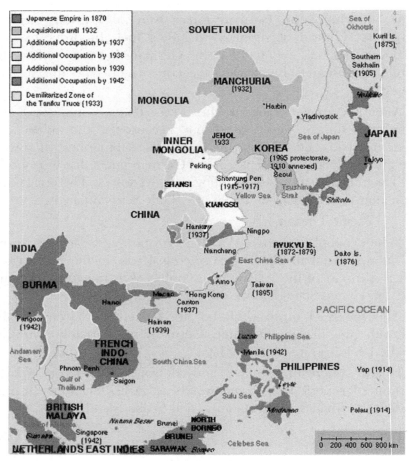

Legend:
- Japanese Empire in 1870
- Acquisitions until 1932
- Additional Occupation by 1937
- Additional Occupation by 1938
- Additional Occupation by 1939
- Additional Occupation by 1942
- Demilitarized Zone of the Tangku Truce (1933)

Japan's empire.

The US was determined to end Japan's control. The Americans took charge of the Allied forces battling in the Pacific theater and began to organize counteroffensives against Japan, leading to a series of battles.

One of the major conflicts to take place in the Pacific theater was the Battle of Iwo Jima. It was fought between Japan and the US and is one of the deadliest battles ever fought by the US Marine Corps.

In 1942, the Joint Chief of Staff (JCOS) was established and put in charge of directing the war effort. The JCOS was made up of officers from the US Air Force, Navy, and Army, with General

Douglas MacArthur and Admiral Chester Nimitz commanding one-half of the Pacific theater.

The two leaderships meant a divided opinion on how the US should advance into the Japanese homeland. MacArthur believed the best way forward was to head toward Tokyo and regain the Philippines on the way, while Nimitz wanted to focus on regaining smaller islands throughout the Pacific. After much discussion, it was decided in 1944 that a combination of both strategies would be used against Japan.

In October 1944, MacArthur took his troops to the Philippines, while Nimitz took control of the Mariana Islands, leading to the significant destruction of Japan's air force and navy.

One of the JCOS officers, General Henry Arnold, felt the Bonin Islands—over two dozen small volcanic islands scattered throughout the central Pacific Ocean—could be the key to attacking Tokyo via air raids. Iwo Jima was ideally placed, as it was located between Tokyo and the Mariana Islands.

Battle of Iwo Jima – February 19th to March 26th, 1945

Arnold had initially planned to take the island of Formosa (present-day Taiwan), but his admirals felt Iwo Jima and Okinawa might be a better bet instead. Once the plan was approved by JCOS, Nimitz began to plan the invasion, which would become known as Operation Detachment.

Iwo Jima was a tiny, volcanic island covered in sand and ash. It contained hundreds of small caves and two airfields named Motoyama 1 and 2. Lieutenant General Kuribayashi Tadamichi was put in charge of defending Iwo Jima. Japan was determined that, win or lose, it would make the US troops suffer.

Tadamichi first built a network of tunnels on the island and then set up blockhouses and gun sites aboveground for protection. His soldiers were stationed either in the caves or the tunnels. The plan was to get the American soldiers deep inland and then attack through a barrage of artillery and infantry fire. Tadamichi also ordered the troops to forego the traditional banzai charge—the Japanese battle cry—and instead use their hideouts to kill as many American soldiers as possible.

When the US finally began its invasion, the small island had over twenty-one thousand Japanese soldiers ready to attack and fend off the invaders.

On the American side, Operation Detachment was made up of naval forces and Marines. They had eleven warships and approximately seventy thousand troops. American intelligence believed the island was being defended by thirteen thousand Japanese troops and were confident that the invasion could be successfully won in four days.

General Joel Alan Schmidt, who was commanding the Marines, had put in a request to bomb Iwo Jima for ten days in a row in preparation for the invasion. He got permission for three due to the narrow timeframe. Nimitz was aiming for a quick win before turning his attention to Okinawa.

The bombing did not go as planned. The weather did not cooperate, and the bombings hardly made a dent on the well-protected island. When the Marines began to land on the island on the morning of February 19th, 1945, they were expecting a quick and efficient landing. But the shore was surrounded by volcanic ash, making the landing more difficult than anticipated. Bulldozers were sent by the US Navy to clear the ash, and they began to make some progress.

Pressing his advantage, Tadamichi ordered his troops to start firing on the confused, disoriented soldiers. A few days after the landing, Tadamichi launched kamikaze attacks on navy vessels. These attacks were a type of suicide attack via bombing with the goal of destroying enemy warships; this same type of attack was used at Pearl Harbor. A Japanese fighter pilot would take their kamikaze aircraft, which was basically a plane that had been converted into a missile, and crash into a ship. More often than not, the ship and the aircraft would explode, leading to complete destruction or severe damage.

A kamikaze attack on the USS Essex during operation in the Pacific theater, 1944.

https://commons.wikimedia.org/wiki/File:USS_Essex_(CV-9)_is_hit_by_a_Kamikaze_off_the_Philippines_on_25_November_1944.jpg

Tadamichi's kamikaze attacks severely damaged some of the American ships, but the US Marines pressed on, undeterred. By February 23rd, the 28th Regiment managed to secure Mount Suribachi, firmly announcing their win by raising an American flag on the summit.

The raising of the American flag on Mount Suribachi.

https://en.wikipedia.org/wiki/File:Raising_the_Flag_on_Iwo_Jima,_larger_-_edit1.jpg

This image has become one of the most enduring and famous images from WWII.

In the meantime, the other regiments continued to advance forward, but their progress was hampered by the extremely strong Japanese defense. American troops were fired upon relentlessly. The US suffered heavy casualties, but little by little, they managed to gain control of some key areas, including Hills 362A and 362B.

By March 10th, the Amphitheater and Turkey Knob were under US control. Less than a week later, on March 16th, the US announced that the last of the Japanese defenses had crumbled and that the invasion of Iwo Jima had been a success.

However, this would not be entirely true until March 26th. On that day, several hundred Japanese troops killed one hundred sleeping Allied troops and then committed suicide. After this, the invasion was considered over, but it came at a very steep cost. Japan lost approximately 18,500 soldiers. Close to 7,000 US Marines died, with another 19,200 wounded.

Nearly every single Japanese soldier was killed or committed suicide, a testament to their unyielding loyalty to their country. The realization that the Japanese would rather die than surrender would go on to influence Harry Truman's decision to bomb Hiroshima and Nagasaki.

The cost for the Americans was high, but the victory benefited them. Iwo Jima's airfields were used for the rest of the war.

Battle of Okinawa – April 1st, 1945 to June 22nd, 1945

As planned by Nimitz, within days of winning the Battle of Iwo Jima, the focus turned to Okinawa. Pre-invasion bombings were started by the US Navy on March 24th, 1945. They continued until March 31st, and on April 1st, 1945, over sixty thousand American troops and Marines stormed the beaches of Okinawa, officially beginning the battle.

This would be the last planned island battle. Okinawa was one of the larger islands. If the Allies could successfully gain control of it, they would have an airbase from where they could launch air strikes on Japan. The island would also provide a base for the Allied fleets and help them blockade important routes for Japan.

The codename for the battle of Okinawa was Operation Iceberg.

The initial landings by the American forces went smoothly, and they met with no resistance from the Japanese troops. However, this would soon change. Much like at Iwo Jima, the Japanese troops put up a fierce and determined defense.

Also like Iwo Jima, Okinawa was not a quick and easy victory. The battle took place over a period of almost three months. Some of the deadliest kamikaze attacks were seen during this battle, destroying or crippling thirty-four US ships.

Okinawa was also the first time when the Japanese began to use *baka*, a suicide weapon like the kamikaze planes. The glider was loaded with explosives and powered by rockets. A Japanese pilot was tasked with guiding the glider to its target and hitting it. A series of offensives and counteroffensives throughout the months of April, May, and June saw the US troops slowly gain ground.

Back home in the US, in the midst of the battle, President Franklin Delano Roosevelt died. Harry Truman became president.

Finally, by June 22nd, the American forces managed to overwhelm and defeat the Japanese, bringing the Battle of Okinawa to a close. Yet again, the US suffered heavy losses. It is estimated that twelve thousand soldiers died, with an additional thirty-six thousand wounded.

Reminiscent of Iwo Jima, many of the Japanese troops chose to kill themselves instead of surrendering.

Japan's Surrender

Once the Battle of Okinawa ended, the Allied powers began to plan the invasion of Japan. Germany had already surrendered, bringing the war in Europe to an end, and the Allies were hoping the same would happen with Japan.

However, the Potsdam Declaration (the Proclamation Defining Terms of Japanese Surrender) was not accepted as planned.

In the declaration, the Allies demanded Japan's unconditional surrender and the complete disarmament of the country's military. It also outlined the intention of trying the Japanese for war crimes and the intent to establish a democratic government in the country. If Japan agreed to the points, it would be allowed to maintain any and all industries that were not related to the war. Furthermore, it would be given access to raw materials and, over time, be allowed to trade internationally again.

However, if they refused to surrender or agree to the terms, the Allies would carry out an aerial and naval attack.

Shortly before the Potsdam Conference was set to begin, Truman received word that the Manhattan Project scientists had successfully carried out a test of the first atomic bomb. He passed the information along to Stalin and outlined his plan to use it should Japan refuse to surrender.

As we know, Japan rejected the Potsdam Declaration. Japan's war minister Korechika Anami said the terms were dishonorable and refused to accept them, thus sealing the fates of Nagasaki and Hiroshima.

Soon after, Truman made the decision to drop the atomic bombs as a way of bringing the war to a swift and final end. Although the decision is heavily criticized to this day by many, it is quite likely that the events of the battles of Iwo Jima and Okinawa heavily influenced Truman's decision.

He firmly believed that by bombing the two cities and forcing Japan to surrender, he had prevented the deaths of thousands of American troops. If previous battles were anything to go by, Japanese troops would choose death as long as it meant taking Allied lives with them.

Truman perhaps felt that he had one shot at crippling Japan completely, and he took it. If he hadn't, would Japan have continued with their kamikaze and baka attacks? Impossible to say for sure, but it is quite likely. However, others have said that Japan was on its last legs, which means the war likely would have concluded without the use of such extreme force.

Whether it was a good call or not, the bombings led to Japan's unconditional surrender and its acceptance of the Potsdam Declaration.

Chapter 6: The War on Land

Life in the Trenches

It's no secret that war is very often glorified. In books, movies, art, and even music, fighting for an ideological cause is seen as the ultimate glory. There are images and stories of camaraderie, of troops marching through lush, green fields, shoulder to shoulder, fighting for a just cause.

However, the reality is very different. Land warfare was absolutely horrendous. It was physically, mentally, and psychologically draining and damaging.

British soldiers in the trenches.

https://ww2db.com/image.php?image_id=5769

World War II was a devastating war, shocking in its bloody savagery. It was by far the most destructive conflict ever witnessed by the world.

The Germans perfected the science of the blitzkrieg. It was a fast-paced, efficient way of invading, destroying, and occupying. Each country the Germans invaded was taken completely by surprise and bombed into submission. This highly effective method accounted for Germany's series of successful invasions at the start of the war. But as Great Britain and the Allies organized themselves, the German forces had a harder time finding victory.

As the Axis and Allies began to battle each other, what followed was one of history's deadliest periods. Bombs were dropped left and right, destroying entire cities. Whatever the bombs might have missed were ravaged by the massive tanks that rolled through the streets. At this point in history, technology was quite advanced, and each side had an arsenal of sophisticated weaponry at their disposal.

The troops fought with a wide array of weapons, such as the following:

- Guns, including rifles, shotguns, submachine guns, and pistols;
- Grenades and mines;
- Machine guns;
- Missiles;
- Poison gas;
- Tanks, including tank destroyers and flame tanks;
- Artillery, such as anti-tank guns, self-propelled guns, rocket launchers, and heavy mortars;
- Atomic bombs;
- Simple things like knives and blades.

A good portion of the battle was fought on foot, with soldiers either on horses or marching on the ground. If an enemy shot at a soldier, mortally wounding them, chances were high that they would die right there on the spot. Those who were lucky were sent back home for a proper burial. Hundreds of thousands of soldiers would never return home again.

Life of a Soldier

The life of a soldier at the front was hardly the romantic experience depicted in books and movies. It was also rather different than military training. Life on the front was unpredictable, traumatic, and potentially deadly.

People who registered for military service were sent to basic training to develop skills and receive training in military life, the chain of command, and weaponry. Depending on what the soldier wanted to do, specialized training might follow basic training. For instance, some people were trained for combat, while others were taught how to operate radios and transmit codes.

Since a large portion of WWII was fought on land, the soldiers who fought on the ground had a tougher experience. Once they were thoroughly trained, they were taken to a holding camp to await further instructions and for their heavy equipment to arrive. The camps were the calm before the storm. There was food, companionship, and a bunk to sleep in at night. And if a soldier was lucky enough to arrive during the warm months, they would find camp life was infinitely more pleasant.

When they finally had to move on, each soldier was given a pack to carry everything they would need to survive: food, clothes, personal items, boots, and helmets, just to name a few things. A separate bag with ammunition and weapons was also carried. In total, each soldier was carrying roughly eighty additional pounds with him at all times. The soldiers also carried a rifle and other items that were distributed amongst them.

The squads of soldiers then marched to their destination, led by a junior officer and sergeants. As they marched, they were acutely aware that enemy forces could be lurking nearby, ready to take them out.

Most of these soldiers had very little idea of what was actually happening with the war. Were they losing? Winning? Nobody knew for sure. Some of the updates that would eventually reach their ears were weeks old.

Depending on where they were headed and the weather, these marches could be horrendous. Soldiers had to slog through mud, rain, ice, scorching heat, or knee-deep snow. There was no respite from the weather, and for those going over mountainous terrain or through dense woods, the march was even more miserable.

Soldiers often ended up with painful blisters on their feet or got trench foot, which happens when your feet are wet for a long period of time. The men had little opportunity to bathe or shave, often going for months without an opportunity to properly clean themselves or wear fresh clothes. Some showers were taken using a bag that was hung several feet off the ground. There would be just enough water in the bag to allow the soldier to soap up and rinse off.

When the soldiers finally reached their destination, they had to set up a camp for the night. Camp consisted of foxholes that had to be dug up individually using an ax or a pick. This was back-breaking work, especially if the ground was frozen and rock-hard. Craters could sometimes be found as a result of artillery; the men would use these craters as camps.

In the winter, soldiers slept in sleeping bags, but most soldiers did not like using them since it made them less mobile. There was always the fear they would be attacked at night.

Even the camps were never truly safe. If they were close to an enemy camp, soldiers were forbidden from smoking or lighting a fire. Some were assigned to patrol at night, while others slept or at least tried to sleep. Soldiers had to get up at dawn and be ready for an attack at any moment from the enemy camp.

The battles themselves were bloody, dangerous, and violent. Most infantrymen carried an M1 Garand semi-automatic rifle, a tough, reliable weapon. This rifle had an eight-round clip that could be fired just by pressing on the trigger for each shot and could even be converted into a grenade launcher!

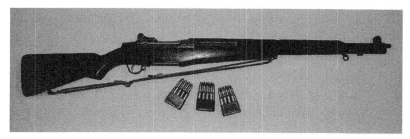

M1 Garand semi-automatic rifle.

Wounded soldiers were treated on the field by a medic, if the squad even had one. Soldiers with severe wounds were sent to a surgical post or a hospital.

Through the course of these sometimes very long battles, soldiers barely had time to think or process anything that was going on except for the enemy before them. They did what they had to do; if they were lucky, they were able to get some rest and maybe a bite to eat before battling the enemy again.

On and on it continued, night and day, until the enemy was vanquished. And then the squad would march to their next stop. Along the way, they would witness horrifying things. They would see the dead bodies of their friends and allies, villages razed to the ground, and innocent civilians killed or wounded. Day in and day out, they lived this horror until the war finally ended.

As we can see, life on the front was not easy or filled with glory. The description above was a basic rundown of a soldier's journey; the actual details were much worse. It is lucky for the world that men were willing to live through this and fight for a just cause because it was not an easy feat.

Key Land Battles during WWII

World War II was fought mainly on land through a series of battles scattered throughout Europe and other parts of the world. While every battle contributed to the war effort, some battles were more decisive than others.

Here is a short list of the most important land battles.

- Operation Barbarossa (June 22nd-December 5th, 1941): This was the German invasion of the Soviet Union. It resulted in the Soviets entering the war on the side of the Allies. After a series of mishaps and heavy losses, the Soviets would end up playing a key role in defeating Germany and the Axis.

- Siege of Leningrad (September 8th, 1941-January 27th, 1944): The city would be under siege by the Germans for nearly nine hundred days. The lifting of the siege was seen as a huge victory for the Soviets and a turning point in the war.

- Battle of Stalingrad (August 23rd, 1942-February 2nd, 1943): Germany's invasion of Stalingrad was met with fierce resistance by the Red Army. The German Army was soundly defeated.

- Battle of Normandy (June 6th-August 30th, 1944): This battle is often seen as the beginning of the end. With Normandy, the Allied troops were able to start pushing the Germans out of France, liberating the country.

- Battle of the Ardennes (December 16th, 1944-January 25th, 1945): Germany's last great offensive and attempt to destroy the Allies initially began with a lot of promise. Germany even believed it could reverse its losing streak, but in the end, the Americans' persistence paid off. The German offensive was pushed back and wrecked.

- Battle of Berlin (April 16th-May 2nd, 1945): This battle spelled the end for Hitler and the Nazis. The Red Army fought fearlessly and captured Berlin while waiting for American reinforcements to arrive. Hitler committed suicide during this battle when he finally came to the realization that Germany had lost.

Additional details and a more in-depth look at these battles can be found in other sections and chapters of this book.

Propaganda and Conscription

Propaganda played a huge and important role in World War II, especially in Nazi Germany.

Various types of propaganda were used to sway civilians to a certain way of thinking. While propaganda helped to increase support for the war and gain troops, conscription was one of the primary ways in which each country was able to enlarge its armies.

Germany

Nazi propaganda would become so strong and effective that people were more than willing to join the Nazi cause, but before they arrived at this stage, Hitler got troops by reintroducing conscription. The announcement for conscription was made on March 16th, 1935.

Hitler stated his plans for Germany's rearmament program and the need to increase the German Army to over half a million troops. The German military would also be renamed Wehrmacht, and the Wehrmacht High Command would be responsible for overseeing the air force, the army, and the navy.

When world leaders began to question Hitler's moves, he assured them he was doing this for defensive purposes and that all Germany wanted was peace. Of course, this was not true. Within a year of reintroducing conscription, the buffer zone between France and Germany was swarming with German soldiers.

The skies above the Rhineland—the buffer zone—were covered with German fighter planes. Hitler's generals felt nervous and worried that France or Great Britain might object since doing this was in direct violation of the Treaty of Versailles. Hitler correctly surmised that they would do nothing.

Over the next three years, Hitler waited, biding his time. He built his armies through conscription. Between 1935 and 1939, 1.3 million men were drafted, and an additional 2.4 million joined the military voluntarily, including women. Over half a million women were volunteer uniformed auxiliaries in the Wehrmacht. Additional volunteers served in aerial defense, nursing, and other units.

When Hitler felt he was ready, he struck.

The United States

In the United States, conscription is typically referred to as "the draft" and has been used a total of six times throughout history for major conflicts, such as the Civil War and WWI.

In 1940, after Germany's successful invasion of France, the general consensus among Americans was that young men should be drafted and begin training just in case. Even though the government wasn't interested in declaring war, there was still worry that the US might be in danger.

The Selective Training and Service Act was signed by Franklin D. Roosevelt, requiring men between the ages of twenty-one and thirty-five to register. The plan was to cap the number of conscripts to 900,000 men, and they would only have to serve for one year unless anything changed. The initial one-year date would be amended once the war was underway.

Voluntary enlistment was closed through Executive Order 9279 one year after Pearl Harbor. Instead, the military chose troops from the Selective Service System.

The draft was active from 1940 to 1946 and was highly successful, with forty-nine million men registering for duty throughout the course of the war. More than ten million men would go on to active military service.

WWII poster in the US encouraging people to enlist.

https://commons.wikimedia.org/wiki/File;J._M._Flagg,_I_Want_You_for_U.S._Army _poster_(1917).jpg

Great Britain

Conscription was imposed in Great Britain immediately after the country declared war on Germany. Within hours of the declaration, Parliament passed the National Service (Armed Forces) Act, requiring men between eighteen to forty-one years old to sign up for the military.

There were, of course, some exceptions. For instance, men who were physically unable to fight were exempt. Men who had essential jobs were also exempt. The Act led to a significant increase in the number of British troops.

Two years after the first National Service Act was passed, Parliament passed another one, this one aimed at women between twenty and thirty years of age. The practice of conscription in Great Britain ended in 1963 and is no longer used.

Chapter 7: The War in the Sky

Aircraft played a huge role in WWII. In many ways, it was the first aerial war. Aircraft worked with and supported the naval and land forces and served a wide variety of purposes beyond dropping bombs on cities.

In this chapter, we will look at the role of aircraft in the war and how it was used by both sides. We will look also take a brief look at the different air force groups.

Luftwaffe

The Luftwaffe was Germany's aerial branch and was established before the start of WWII. Germany's previous air force had been dismantled, as per the conditions of the Treaty of Versailles.

When Hitler came into power, he reestablished the air force. The Luftwaffe fell under the purview of the Wehrmacht High Command.

By 1939, the Luftwaffe was extremely advanced. It was the latest, greatest thing in terms of technology, and when Poland was invaded, it quickly became evident just how superior the Luftwaffe was.

The invasions of Norway and France were successful because of the Luftwaffe's contribution; in fact, the Luftwaffe helped get Germany over seventy thousand air victories during the war. The Luftwaffe bombed both military and non-military targets, resulting in the deaths of thousands of innocent civilians. The hardest hit was the Soviet Union.

However, as the war continued, there was a visible weakening of the Luftwaffe, and it began to lose its superiority. Its effectiveness also began to decline steadily. After a particularly spectacular loss during Operation Bodenplatte (an operation that targeted the Low Countries) on January 1ˢᵗ, 1945, the Luftwaffe was no longer considered to be useful or effective.

One of the Luftwaffe's major flaws was the lack of a solid air defense system. The war in Germany began before the Luftwaffe's defenses were complete. This meant it had to develop defenses on the go while fighting a war. There was also a problematic lack of communication between the various flying branches, which, in turn, resulted in poor coordination.

Just over a year after the invasion of Poland, the Luftwaffe was dealing with heavy losses. They badly needed new aircraft but were bogged down by production issues, partially as a result of poor planning and partially due to not having enough resources. Germany was unable to develop the technology further, again due to supply issues and the lack of access to raw materials such as aluminum or oil. This greatly hampered the war effort.

The Luftwaffe played a rather sinister role in the concentration camps, namely Auschwitz and Dachau, where prisoners were used as subjects for experiments for the Luftwaffe. For example, in one of the experiments, prisoners were used to figure out at what altitude someone could be ejected safely from their seats.

When the war finally ended, several Luftwaffe commanders were put on trial for the crimes they had committed during the war.

Similar to Japan's kamikaze, a special task force within the Luftwaffe called the Sonderkommando carried out attacks on air where aircraft were purposely used to attack Allied bombers mid-air, causing them to explode. More often than not, the pilots on these missions died.

Japanese Imperial Air Force

Japan's air force was named the Imperial Japanese Army Air Service (IJAAS). While Japanese aviation played a role in WWI, the Japanese government only began to take the development of military aviation seriously after the war ended. They quickly realized how advantageous it would be to develop new technologies, so they got to work.

An aircraft factory was built in 1916. At first, Japan was using the services of people like Dr. Richard Vogt, an engineer from Germany, to create designs for them.

Imperial Japanese Air Force Mitsubishi Ki-21-II bombers.

https://commons.wikimedia.org/wiki/File:Mitsubishi_Ki_21-2s.jpg

By the late 1920s, they were producing their own designs, and several years after that, they had created an extensive collection of aircraft.

The Imperial Air Force was recognized as a distinct yet equal branch to the Imperial Army's other branches of the military: the cavalry, the infantry, and the artillery.

By the time WWII was well underway, in 1941, Japan's Imperial Air Force was made up of 1,500 aircraft, with the country continuously developing new technology. The aircraft they used for combat were incredibly advanced machines. They utilized fighter planes, bombers, transports, trainers, and reconnaissance planes, to name a few.

One of the deadliest aspects of the Japanese air force was the kamikaze pilots. These pilots were essentially given a suicide mission and used to destroy important posts. They were used more extensively by Japan toward the end of the war.

Even though Japan started strong, Japan's air force was unable to maintain momentum. They didn't have enough aircraft. Poor planning and limited cooperation between the army, navy, and air forces also contributed to Japan's failures as the war progressed.

Like Germany, Japan was having production difficulties. They couldn't replace the aircraft fast enough to make up for their heavy losses. They also did not have enough pilots to man the aircraft. And as existing pilots began to be killed or wounded in battle, their situation worsened.

Difficulties finding resources like fuel and mechanics didn't help matters either.

After the war was lost and Japan was defeated, the Imperial Air Force, navy, and army were disbanded.

Soviet Air Forces

The Soviet Union was very strong and capable on many fronts; however, their air force was not one of them. In fact, the Soviets had one of the weakest aerial forces, which is ironic given that in 1938, the Soviet Union's air force was the largest one in the world. However, the planes were poorly designed, not the most technologically advanced, and not prepared for a war in any way.

Soviet engineers had been more focused on creating bomber planes, which were loud, showy, and could fly really far, instead of developing planes that would be good for tactical warfare.

Along with the bomber and attack planes, the Soviet Air Forces also had fighter planes, transport planes, trainers, and reconnaissance and patrol aircraft. But none of these aircraft were particularly advanced. Stalin himself admitted in the early 1930s that the Soviet military was lagging decades behind in terms of modernization.

The Yak 9 aircraft.

As a result of this poor planning and poor organization, the Soviet Union was woefully unprepared for Germany's invasion in 1941. A week after the invasion, roughly four thousand Soviet aircraft had been decimated by the Luftwaffe.

The Soviets also experienced a significant lack of pilots and other support crews to man the aircraft. A program was created during the war that allowed women with prior flying experience or training to engage in air combat.

When the Lend-Lease Act was launched in March 1941, the Soviets were able to receive US-built aircraft. They received nearly fifteen thousand aircraft under the program. These far more sophisticated and powerful aircraft went a long way toward helping the Soviet Army during the war.

The Soviet Union also began to increase its production of aircraft. As a result, between 1941 and 1945, it produced over 157,000 machines, the majority of which were built for combat.

After the war ended and the Cold War began, the Soviet Union's focus turned to creating and developing the newest, most advanced technologies for its military, with an emphasis on its aircraft.

United States Army Air Forces (AAF)

The AAF was established on June 20th, 1941, and fell under the umbrella of the United States Army. The AAF was the country's aerial warfare service, and it was disbanded after the end of the war.

In 1938, Germany's Luftwaffe began to play a more prominent role by supporting ground forces in German-occupied Czechoslovakia and Sudetenland. President Franklin D. Roosevelt realized that Europe may have been dragged into another war and that the US might have to get involved. In order to win the war, the US would need a strong air force.

A year later, Roosevelt received $300 million USD to establish an air corps. When Hitler began his invasions in Europe, the air corps began to rapidly expand, as new bases were established in the US and overseas.

The air force had an extensive collection of various aircraft for different missions and purposes. The most common ones used for combat included bomber planes; fighter planes; observation, transport, and trainer planes; and utility, glider, and rescue planes.

The AAF was extremely organized, and over the course of the war, it only got stronger and more powerful. Within a period of three years (1942 to 1945), the US produced nearly 275,000 aircraft! This number was higher than the total number of aircraft produced by Japan, Germany, and Great Britain.

From the moment the US joined the war until the end, the AAF played a critical role in helping win battles and victories. They dropped bombs, conducted air raids, engaged in air-to-air combat, brought supplies for ground troops, defended the airs, and provided support to naval and ground support.

During D-Day, the AAF played an important role by clearing the path for troops to land and invade Normandy. To reduce combat fatigue, the AAF made sure to replace and rotate crews frequently to give their pilots and air personnel a break.

The AAF's organization, communication, experienced crew, and ability to produce hundreds of aircraft made it the most powerful and superior air force on the battlefield. With the AAF's help, the Allies ended up with a far more destructive air force. In 1947, the United States would create a permanent air force.

The Royal Air Force (RAF)

Great Britain's air force is called the Royal Air Force or RAF for short. It was established in 1918, and by the end of WWI, the RAF had become the world's largest air force. During WWII, the RAF played a hugely important role, especially during the Battle of Britain.

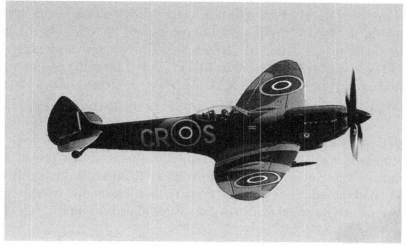

The Supermarine Spitfire Mk XVI NR.

Chowells/Noise reduction and shadows lifted by Diliff., CC BY-SA 2.5 <https://creativecommons.org/licenses/by-sa/2.5>, via Wikimedia Commons; https://commons.wikimedia.org/wiki/File:Supermarine_Spitfire_Mk_XVI_NR.jpg

Before the start of and during WWII, the RAF was considerably expanded. Like most of the countries embroiled in the war, the RAF's aircraft included fighters and bomber planes, torpedo and dive bombers, level bombers, patrol and reconnaissance planes, trainers, and transport planes.

During the war, one of the RAF's primary focuses was an offensive bombing campaign against Germany. The RAF wanted to make sure Germany was weak and unable to fight as efficiently. The RAF's contributions to the war helped the Allies win numerous victories and ultimately end the war.

The contribution from the RAF also included female fighter pilots who joined the war effort. In January 1940, there were only eight women who were part of the effort, but within a few very short years, over 165 women pilots were flying fighter planes and spitfires.

The Battle of Britain

The RAF's single greatest victory during the war is likely the Battle of Britain, which it won singlehandedly.

After a series of stunning German victories, including the fall of France, Hitler turned his eye on Great Britain, invading it in July 1940. He expected a quick victory.

However, the RAF managed to successfully defend Great Britain from the Luftwaffe's relentless bombings and air raids. No matter what the Germans did, the RAF's superior aircraft and strategies could not be broken through. Over 1,700 Luftwaffe planes were shot down by the RAF. The RAF lost about 1,250 aircraft.

When Germany began to lose aircraft at an alarming pace, Hitler was forced to give up and turn his attention elsewhere. The battle ended on October 31ˢᵗ. This would be the first serious loss for Germany, which had only tasted success up until that point. The Luftwaffe was never quite able to recover from these losses. If the RAF had failed, it is almost certain that Germany would have invaded and occupied Great Britain as it did with France.

Chapter 8: The War in the Media

Propaganda

Regardless of which side of the war one was on, the propaganda used to conscript people were similar. Each side had strong ideological beliefs, and each portrayed the other side as the enemy.

Nazi Propaganda

One of the most powerful and important tools in Adolf Hitler's meteoric rise to power was propaganda. He and the Nazi Party used it extremely effectively, legitimating the party and increasing party membership. The skillful use of propaganda is what helped Hitler get elected, and it's what he used to eventually become a dictator.

In order to connect to the masses, Hitler's focus was on relaying clear and simple messages that appealed to the wider public while exploiting their fears. Hitler's timing was impeccable, as Germany's economy had tanked. People around the world were living through the Great Depression, but Germany was severely hit because of the terms implemented by the Treaty of Versailles.

For example, one of Hitler's messages that targeted the working-class people was "Bread and Work." This message tapped into people's fears and instability surrounding the lack of employment, wages, and food shortages.

Another message, "Mother and Child," showed what the Nazi idea of a woman was.

One of Hitler's most trusted advisors was Joseph Goebbels. He joined the party early on, doing so in 1924. Goebbels would become the force behind the Nazis' highly successful propaganda machine. He was so successful that he became the Minister of Propaganda in 1933.

Goebbels used a combination of various types of media, such as art, posters, film, music, radio, and newspapers. He worked hard to reach the maximum number of people. He also carefully began to craft Hitler's image, turning him almost into a mythical leader who was strong and powerful. A leader who would be Germany's savior, who would help the country get back on its feet.

Hitler promised jobs and economic recovery and assured the people that Germany would rise once again with his guiding hand at the helm.

As you can imagine, the "Hitler myth" was highly successful and very effective.

The methods of propaganda that led to Hitler's rise to power were later used to portray the Jewish people as the enemy, an enemy that would be the downfall of Germany.

Hitler recognized the key role propaganda played in his rise. Once he became the chancellor of Germany, he established the Ministry of Public Enlightenment and Propaganda. This in itself was a brilliant move since governments typically only organized committees to spread propaganda while at war. By establishing the ministry during a time of peace, Hitler further legitimatized what he was doing.

Goebbels, who was put in charge of the ministry, envisioned Germany as an enormous empire with absolute control over the people's education and beliefs, as well as the media. He used the anger most Germans felt about their defeat in World War I and emphasized national pride.

In Goebbels's own words, "The essence of propaganda consists in winning people over to an idea so sincerely, so vitally, that in the end they succumb to it utterly and can never again escape from it."[8]

One of the propaganda ministry's first moves was to gain control of the guild that allowed journalists and editors to get jobs. On October 4th, 1933, after gaining control of the Reich Association of the German Press, a new law requiring all journalists and editors to be pure of race was passed without protest. The Editors Law would be the start of a long campaign that banished Jewish people from nearly every aspect of German society.

Under the ministry's governance, the press had to follow mandates and laws passed by the ministry. The press could not print or put out anything that might make Hitler's regime look weak to the German people or the world. The news was controlled even further when daily guidelines and directives on what should be written and how they should be written were issued from Berlin and sent to the offices of local papers.

What happened if anyone defied these directives? They were sent to a concentration camp. Before long, everyone was doing exactly what they were instructed to do. Opposition newspapers were forcefully shut down, while any media or publishing businesses owned by Jewish people were taken away from them and given to "racially pure" Germans. Within months, the idea of a free press had evaporated. The Nazis now controlled everything from the radio to the theater, and they used all these mediums to advance their ideologies and beliefs.

During the war itself, propaganda was used extensively by the Nazis to depict the German Army as a brave, powerful, and conquering force fighting for German nationality. In sharp contrast, Soviet troops were portrayed as heartless, inhumane machines who felt no fear. The Allied powers were misguided cowards who didn't know any better.

Over time, people were brainwashed to believe all these things were true. And more horrifying still, most believed that Jews were evil and did not deserve to live. Nazi propaganda encouraged and ignited hatred in the people's hearts toward Jews and others who

---

[8] "World War II Propaganda."
https://www.pbs.org/wgbh/americanexperience/features/goebbels-propaganda/.

were not of the Aryan race.

So, when hundreds of thousands of Jews, Romani, Soviet prisoners of war, and other Nazi victims were shipped off to concentration camps, most people were either indifferent or felt relieved. Very few people had the courage to fight back against what the Nazis were feeding them.

Propaganda's "task is not to make an objective study of the truth, in so far as it favors the enemy, and then set it before the masses with academic fairness; its task is to serve our own right, always and unflinchingly."[9] This was written by Hitler in his book *Mein Kampf*, and it perfectly captures what the Nazis did and why they did it. They twisted the media and used propaganda to serve Hitler's cause.

British Propaganda

When WWII broke out, Great Britain once more reestablished the Ministry of Information that had been set up for WWI. The purpose of the ministry was to create propaganda that would rally the population together and provide support to the troops and the war effort.

Like Germany, Great Britain also used a mix of modern and traditional media, including films and leaflets. While much of the propaganda was filled with hostility for the Axis powers, especially Germany, the general themes of the advertisements or posters were more positive or motivational than those put out by Goebbels. Emphasis was placed on supporting the Allies, fighting for freedom, and being brave. Each civilian was supposed to do their own part to help the war effort.

People were encouraged to be frugal, grow vegetables, and volunteer for work that could be done within the country. Women were pushed to join the Land Army or the ATS (Auxiliary Territorial Service) or work in munitions factories. In short, everyone was made to feel they had a role to play during the war, whether at the front or at home, and that winning the war depended on everyone pulling together.

---

[9] "Hitler on Propaganda." http://fcit.usf.edu/holocaust/resource/document/docpropa.htm.

A British propaganda poster encouraging women to join the war effort.

https://commons.wikimedia.org/wiki/File:Kriegsplakate_6_db.jpg

A lot of the propaganda was devoted to making people feel good about the war effort. Every German defeat and every victory by the British forces were joyfully announced to boost the country's morale and assure the people the Allies were headed down the right path. No matter what was happening, British propaganda tried to focus on the positive. When the tide started to turn for the Allies, British propaganda and radio commentaries became even more inspirational.

Much of the government's information about the war was relayed through propaganda, such as encouraging children to be sent away from the city and how to stay safe during a blackout or air raid.

And, of course, there was the propaganda related to why the British were fighting the war. The issue was depicted simply: it was a fight between light versus darkness, good versus evil.

Hitler was an evil that needed to be rooted out, and the Allies were the ones responsible for doing so, not only to help themselves but also to save the world. As the war went on, the tone shifted. Images and accounts of the war became more sinister to increase the dislike and hatred for the Germans and the Axis powers.

British propaganda about Hitler.

Sentiment toward the Japanese was lukewarm. While their actions on the Pacific were seen as deplorable, the main target for hatred continued to be the Germans. However, when recruiting African troops, British propaganda placed greater emphasis on anti-Japanese sentiment since that was the more imminent threat to them. The Italians also did not face the same kind of anger as the Germans.

British propaganda also created specific campaigns to bolster public opinion about the other Allies. For example, after the Battle of Stalingrad, the British put out leaflets and posters about the Soviet Union's great victory, painting the Soviets in a very favorable light.

Much propaganda was aimed at the United States with one goal in mind: to have them join the war. The British were careful not to present it as propaganda; instead, they were delivered as news reports and information. While Franklin D. Roosevelt was keen to join the war effort, the American public wanted nothing to do with it. Both FDR and the British government hoped that news coverage of the battles and the situation in Europe would sway public opinion.

In short, the British used propaganda in a skillful way to bolster morale, gain international support, and provide hope, all while making sure that the people knew exactly who their enemy was.

American Propaganda

As mentioned earlier, President Franklin D. Roosevelt was keen to join the war, but having fought in the First World War, most of the US had no desire to get involved in what they viewed as yet another European problem.

While the British had begun to use propaganda to change American minds, the American government was reluctant to use any type of propaganda, even after they officially joined the war in 1941. This mindset eventually shifted due to increasing pressure from a number of industries that wanted clearer directives, including businesses and the media. When the government began to use propaganda, they wanted to be clear the materials would be used to provide information to the public.

Propaganda was used effectively to garner public sympathy toward the Allied forces and instill a desire within the public to support them. All types of media were used to ignite hatred for Germany and the other Axis powers.

The media of choice for the US seemed to be posters, with the country producing the most posters than any other country engaged in the war. Nearly 200,000 unique posters were designed and printed, mostly with encouraging, supportive messages. For instance, the US made posters of Rosie the Riveter, who was supposed to represent the women joining the workforce.

The woman in this poster was never identified as Rosie the Riveter during the war, although many Americans today mistakenly call her by the name. The poster did not become the famous symbol it is today until the 1960s.

https://en.wikipedia.org/wiki/File:We_Can_Do_It!_NARA_535413_-_Restoration_2.jpg

Advertisements for a number of different causes were released by the country, including selling war bonds, encouraging production in factories, and urging everyone to contribute what they could to the war effort. These advertisements were a key factor in maintaining public morale.

The running theme for most of America's propaganda was patriotism. The Allies were portrayed as the "right" side, while the Axis powers were made to look like weak, cowardly creatures who could not be taken seriously. Hitler was often ridiculed and depicted as a foolish man who was doomed to fail. The Nazi Party was portrayed as the ultimate evil, worse than anything anyone could imagine.

Like Great Britain, the point of the war was simplified to good versus evil. President Roosevelt especially wanted people to understand what a catastrophe it would be if Europe and Asia were ruled by dictators.

In 1942, the Office of War Information was established. The agency would go on to be involved with propaganda in Hollywood movies and other forms of media.

US propaganda poster.

Another organization that was put together to produce and publish propaganda was the Writers' War Board. The board was closely linked to President Roosevelt's administration and established a link between writers and the government. Oftentimes, the writers were far more blistering and took a bolder approach than the government.

Comic book writers also got involved in the war effort to sway people to the "right" side. Superheroes were now battling real-life villains instead of fictional ones.

Advertising played a big role in war propaganda. Companies and big businesses used the war as a way to promote their own brand and what they were doing. Advertisements either supported the war or depicted a company's contribution to the war effort. The companies that could find a way to link their products to the war did so. For example, Coca-Cola advertised that its products were consumed by factory workers and troops. Ads like this supported the war and were good for business. The soldiers at the front also liked getting magazines that were filled with colorful ads. It was a win-win.

Effectiveness of Media

In general, propaganda was spread mainly through modern and traditional media, such as radio programs, newspapers, magazines, films, and posters. In an era where not everyone was exposed to media or had access to media, word of mouth played an important role.

The media was extremely effective at passing on the ideologies and beliefs of the governments and leaders in charge. This was especially true for the Nazi Party. The Nazis had absolute control over every form of media and had complete power over what the population did or did not see. The German population had little access to anything beyond what the Nazi-controlled state told them. Years of being brainwashed by Nazi propaganda is one of the reasons why nobody seemed particularly horrified by the idea of concentration camps or the idea of a supreme Aryan race.

For the Allies, propaganda was effective because it clearly depicted an "evil" that had to be fought by the "good" guys. It helped garner sympathy and support from the population and increased the number of volunteers. Men felt compelled to defend innocent people and rid the world of an evil presence. Women were inspired to step up and take action as well.

Of course, almost every bit of propaganda had some element of untruth to it. Nazi propaganda, for instance, was almost entirely based on lies and fabrications. Allied propaganda was more truthful and factual; however, to keep up morale at home, they worked hard to put a positive spin on what was happening on the front. Most people who were removed from the war had no idea of the actual horrors being endured by those on the battlefield. In the US, the war was often spun in a heroic, glorified way.

Civilians in Europe lived through nightly raids and bombings, so they knew better. Letters sent from soldiers at the front also painted a different picture. For example, one soldier at the front described in a letter back home:

"Our first evidence of actual battle is anything but poetic. Behind a wall-like hedgerow is a series of abandoned foxholes, each surrounded by a litter of used K-ration cartons, tin cans, empty cartridge casings, dried human feces. This has been the front line. It is eloquent of a new reality, the feces perhaps most eloquent. There'd been no time to relieve yourself leisurely, cover your deposit afterward, and no such niceties as toilet paper. Like an animal afraid for your life you jumped out of your hole, excreted, jumped back in. The dead or wounded had of course been removed to the rear long before we passed. The able-bodied had gone forward as we were going. Again the courage and blood of others paved the way."[10]

Adversely, soldiers were reluctant to lay bare the true horrors of the war to their loved ones and often didn't mention anything negative at all. They tried to write brave, happy, positive letters. What follows is an example of such a letter from Private Harry Schiraldi:

"Dear Ma, Just a few lines tonight to let you know that I'm fine and hope everybody at home is in the best of health. I just finished playing baseball and took a nice shower and now I feel very nice. Hope every thing is going alright at home and don't forget if you ever need money you could cash my war bonds anything you want to. This afternoon I went to church and I received Holy

---

[10] "Letters from the Front." https://www.pbs.org/wgbh/americanexperience/features/dday-letters-front/.

Communion again today. Getting holy, ain't I?"[11]

Henry died the following day on D-Day when an enemy machine gun fired on him on the beaches of Normandy.

Propaganda, media, and letters aside, the true horrors of the war were only really revealed once it ended. The terrible truths were laid bare among the rubble, the dead, and the concentration camps.

Each side did what they had to in order to garner support for their cause, and they did it very effectively.

[11] Sharmi, Swati. "A U.S. Soldier's Last Letter Home before He Died on D-Day." https://www.washingtonpost.com/news/worldviews/wp/2014/06/05/a-u-s-soldiers-last-letter-home-before-he-died-on-d-day/

At first glance, World Wa
the Nazi Party. But whe
the major powers we
beliefs.

It was not j
were many
However
signific
fasc

Part Three: Ideology and Involvement

r II was about defeating Adolf Hitler and
n one digs a little deeper, one can see how
re motivated and led by their core ideological

st an ideological war. As discussed in Part One, there
other factors that led to and contributed to the war.
, numerous ideologies were at play that did have a
ant and important influence on the war effort, notably
sm, Nazism, communism, nationalism, and democracy.

Over the next few chapters, we will examine the extent these
ideologies influenced the course of the war.

Chapter 9: Nazism, Hitler, and the Death Camps

What is Nazism?

National Socialism, otherwise known as Nazism, was a totalitarian movement with Adolf Hitler at the helm. It shared a lot of commonalities with Italy's fascism. Both movements appealed to the masses, were led by a dictator who wielded absolute control, and focused on intense nationalism. However, Nazism was more extreme. In many ways, Nazism was the younger, more radical, and more violent brother of fascism.

The roots of Nazism go back much further than Hitler and can partially be linked all the way back to the 1680s. However, for the purpose of this book, we will look at Nazism during Hitler's time.

The Nazi Party has its origins in the German Workers' Party, which was established in 1919. It was a political organization that was made up of anti-Semites who were angry about the humiliation Germany had been subjected to under the Treaty of Versailles. They believed Germany had been treated unfairly by the international world and that the treaty was unacceptable. They focused on promoting German pride while also spreading anti-Semitic beliefs.

Hitler joined this party in 1919. When he became its leader in 1921, the name of the party was changed to Nationalist Social German Worker's Party or, as it would become known throughout the world, the Nazi Party.

Nazis rejected the notions of democracy or liberalism. They did not believe in the concept of human or equal rights or the rule of law. They viewed women as inferior to men, believing their sole purpose in life was to procreate. Nazis also believed the state should rule the people and demanded absolute obedience from them. Above all, they believed that pure Germans or Aryans were not only superior but that they should also control the world. The Nazis' worldview was that the world needed to be purged of racially impure, weak, fragile, and damaged people until only the Aryan race existed.

According to the Nazis, pure Aryans had a Nordic background. They were tall and had pale white skin and blue eyes. Their heads were long and shapely, and they had slim, narrow noses, blond hair, and a defined chin.

One of the Nazi Party's top priorities was to further the Aryan race. They encouraged people who fit the criteria of "strong and pure" to breed and have children together. For example, young people who were planning to get married and have children were eligible for interest-free loans from the Nazi Party. However, they had to prove they came from the Aryan race. Nazis also required the bride to have worked at a job for six months, which she would then quit to get married. In this way, the Nazis were assured of a job vacancy that could be filled by a man.

Couples who received the loan were forgiven one-quarter of the loan for every child they had. It was an incentive for each "perfect" couple to have at least four "perfect" children. They also believed a woman's role was at home as a wife and mother, and this program helped keep them there. This encouragement of procreating to bring more "superior" beings into the world was called "positive eugenics."

"Negative eugenics" was the opposite. It was designed to prevent flawed, disabled, and undesirable people from having children. For instance, in July 1933, the Nazis passed a law giving the government permission to sterilize people who suffered from genetic or hereditary diseases like schizophrenia, deafness, and blindness, just to name a few.

For the Nazis, the next logical step in their obsession with racial cleansing and desire to create a "master race" was eliminating anyone who did not fit the criteria. It, therefore, wasn't a stretch to house non-Aryans in concentration camps and have them exterminated.

Adolf Hitler

The most talked about Nazi is, without a doubt, Adolf Hitler.

He was born on April 20th, 1889, in a small town in Austria. As a little boy, Hitler loved the arts and wanted to become an artist. He applied to the Vienna Academy of the Arts but didn't get in. When he was eighteen, his mother died, and he moved to Vienna, hoping to pursue a career in the arts.

Within a year, Hitler had gone through the substantial money he had inherited from his parents and was living in poverty and sleeping in homeless shelters. His family encouraged him to enter the civil service, but he refused.

Over the next few years, he managed to scrape together enough money to live on by painting the scenery of Vienna. During his time there, he developed relationships with Jewish people, both personally and professionally. In fact, he earned a portion of his living by selling to Jews in Vienna.

While in Vienna, Hitler was strongly influenced by politician Georg Ritter von Schönerer's racist nationalism and the views of the mayor of Vienna, Karl Lueger. Lueger openly promoted anti-Semitic views and reinforced views that Jews were the ultimate threat and Germany's enemy.

At the time, Austria had a universal three-year conscription. Hitler did not want to fight for the Habsburgs. Since he was at risk of getting arrested for shirking his duty, he moved to Munich, Germany, instead. His life continued in much the same way in Munich; he earned a basic living by painting.

And then the First World War broke out. Suddenly, Hitler found a purpose in life. He enlisted voluntarily and joined the Bavarian Regiment. Luck clung to him like a shadow throughout the war, as he managed to escape life-threatening situations time and time again. Hitler didn't have a military bearing and was a loner, but he was an eager soldier. He never took leave and never complained about the conditions.

In 1916, during the Battle of the Somme, Hitler's leg was injured. After a brief recovery at the hospital, he was assigned to other duties in Munich. While he was there, he saw and heard Germans expressing anti-war sentiments and a general sense of indifference. This upset him greatly, and he placed the blame squarely on the Jews, believing they were hampering the war effort.

Hitler asked to return to the thick of the action. He performed extremely well and even received five medals; however, he never progressed past corporal. Ironically, his commanding officers felt he did not have the personality or skills to command respect from the troops or be a leader.

When it started to become clear that Germany was losing the war, Hitler became depressed and spent a lot of time thinking. When the war finally ended, he wasn't on the battlefield but was instead recovering from a gas attack in a hospital. He was devasted by the news of the Kaiser's fall, and seeds of hatred began to grow in his heart for the people who had let down Germany. Again, inexplicably, he blamed the Jews.

Once more, Hitler felt adrift. And then the Nazi Party came along. When the party was founded, Hitler joined as a party member, and within two years, he climbed the ranks to become the party's leader.

In 1923, Hitler, feeling inspired by Mussolini's march on Rome, decided he had had enough of the Weimar Republic. He tried to stage a coup with the Nazi Party's backing to displace the government, but he failed. He was arrested two days later and sentenced to five years in prison. However, he only served nine months. While in prison, he wrote *Mein Kampf.*

Adolf Hitler.

In this autobiographical work, Hitler outlined his views and beliefs on many things, including his deep hatred for communists and Jews. He talked about how he wanted to get rid of parliamentary systems and establish a new world order where the weak and sickly would be exterminated in order to make room in the world for strong, capable people.

The volumes were written mainly for his party, but as his power grew, people began to be interested in what he had to say, and sales began to increase. He made over a million Reichsmarks from his books back then. That would be equivalent to over six million euros today!

As time passed, Hitler's popularity grew. He was well-spoken, utterly mesmerizing, and had a way of appealing to the masses. He used the country's desperate situation to his advantage. He spoke at length about how democracy was to blame for unemployment and the depression. Hitler promised the people prosperity and to get rid of Jewish bankers and financiers who were bringing them down. He spoke with confidence about a new world order under which Germany would no longer be weak or crippled but would rise strong and proud, filled with people of the Aryan race.

The people were hooked. They flocked to the Nazi Party in droves. By 1932 (less than a decade after Hitler's failed coup), the Nazi Party had become the Reichstag's biggest political party.

In 1933, Hitler was appointed chancellor of Germany by President Paul von Hindenburg. He got to work immediately. Almost overnight, civil liberties began to be suppressed. Democratic institutions began to crumble, and anyone who opposed his changes was murdered or taken away.

After Hindenburg's death in 1934, Hitler seamlessly slid into absolute power. He named himself Führer and became the army's commander in chief. The expansion of the army, including a new air force, began quickly, while troops were gathered through the reintroduction of conscription.

Laws and decrees began to be passed against Jewish people, segregating and isolating them from German society and slowly stripping them of their civil rights. These laws would lay the groundwork for what would follow.

The steps Hitler took and the money he spent on the military brought prosperity to the country. He also held up his promise to widen Germany's natural boundaries. The first thing he did was annex Austria. He then forced Czechoslovakia to hand over the Sudetenland.

Since the international world did nothing, Hitler became bolder. The people began to go along with his policies and beliefs since everything he had done so far had been to their advantage. They were convinced he would guide them down the right path.

A year after that, Hitler invaded Poland and started WWII.

The invasion was just the beginning; there would be so much more to come. So many horrors and terrible truths would only be revealed much later.

Nazi Concentration Camps

Concentration camps are commonly associated with the Holocaust; however, the first camp was built by the Nazi Party as soon as Hitler became chancellor in 1933, years before the war began.

Throughout the course of the war, the Nazis would go on to set up over forty-four thousand concentration camps, incarceration camps, and ghettos.

Dachau, the first camp, was set up right outside Munich and used to house political prisoners, including communists and socialists. It would become the model to follow for future camps.

In 1938, the first set of Jewish males was sent to Dachau. After Kristallnacht (the "Night of Broken Glass"), the Nazis began to round up more Jewish men. Over thirty thousand men were held in concentration camps.

The term concentration camp has become synonymous with gas chambers and death, but not all the camps were used for the same purpose. Some camps were used for forced labor, some to house prisoners of war, and some were transit camps where Jewish people were held until they could be deported. More often than not, deportation meant being sent to a killing center.

The Nazis built five killing centers in total. While people died in the other camps too, the killing centers were designed specifically for mass extermination. Hitler and the Nazis were obsessed with the idea of racial superiority and wanted to wipe out the Jews. These camps were the "final solution" to the Jewish problem.

Concentration camps were guarded by the SS (the Schutzstaffel). The SS was a paramilitary organization that evolved from a small guard unit to a police force tasked with security and enforcing the Nazi Party's policies.

Heinrich Himmler inspecting a prisoner.

Deportation

Soon after Kristallnacht and the mass imprisonment of Austrian Jews, Jewish people became the Nazis' main target. The Nazis didn't even try to make up an excuse for arresting them. Being a Jew was crime enough. Nazis began to round up Jewish people and deport them. Most prisoners were told to pack a suitcase and fed lies about where they would be sent. They were always invariably led to believe they would simply be taken outside of Germany and released.

This was, of course, false.

Sometimes, families were deported together. Other times, people were called up randomly. In either case, the prisoner was put on a train headed for a camp.

The journey could take anywhere from a few days to several weeks. The prisoners were crammed together in a boxcar with no room to sit, move, or even kneel. There were no bathroom breaks and no pauses for sleep or rest. They were given very little food to share between them. Pain, hunger, and inhumane conditions led to many deaths during the transport.

The conditions inside these compartments were awful beyond belief, but the worst was still to come.

Camp Life in Auschwitz-Birkenau

While there were many different concentration camps, we will look at the most infamous camp of all, Auschwitz, which was established in 1940. The camp originally served as army barracks for the Polish army and was adapted to serve the Nazis' purpose.

The Nazis added more buildings and second stories to the existing buildings. Every building was meant to house roughly seven hundred prisoners, but the actual number was much higher, well over one thousand.

When the train finally reached the camp, most prisoners felt an immense sense of relief. They had reached the end of their horrifying journey and would now be released. But the minute they stepped out, they were greeted by a massive sign curled around the iron gate that read, *"Arbeit Macht Frei"* ("Work makes one free").

The prisoners were sorted into two groups: one for men and another for women and children. They would then be lined up for inspection. The SS would decide who would live and who would die. Those who looked too weak or sick were sent to the gas chamber while the rest were moved forward for identification.

Each prisoner's suitcase and personal effects would be taken away. The people were assigned a number, which was tattooed on their arms. The registration process also included the assigning of barracks and work.

Once this was complete, the prisoners had to undress so their heads could be shaved. This was followed by a public shower under the ever-watchful eye of the SS. After the shower, they were given blue and white striped pajamas.

Bald, tattooed, and dressed the same, the prisoners were stripped of their individual identity and dignity.

Most prisoners were woken up at four in the morning. They were given a half hour to eat, get dressed, go to the bathroom, and clean their barracks. This was followed by morning roll call, which could sometimes take hours. This was especially harsh during the winter months when prisoners had to stand shivering in the snow and sleet.

After roll call, everyone went to their assigned work. The lucky ones were assigned jobs in the administration building or sorting through clothing and personal belongings, while others were assigned to break rocks or dispose of dead bodies.

Meals were provided but in such small quantities that everyone was malnourished. After working all day, the prisoners were subjected to hours-long roll call again before being given some "free time." Most of the people were so exhausted and weak that they simply went to sleep.

The beds were either wooden planks or mattresses stuffed with straw and laid out on the floor. Most beds were shared by eighteen to twenty people.

Brick bunks at Auschwitz; four prisoners would sleep in one of these partitions.

Disease and illnesses were rampant in the extremely unsanitary conditions of the camp, which were infested with vermin, rats, and lice.

This daily routine was the best the prisoners could hope for. As horrible and inhumane as these conditions were, it was far preferable to the atrocities that befell many prisoners. Throughout the day, the prisoners were watched carefully by the SS and were at the mercy of their whims and desires. For the bored SS guards, torturing the prisoners was something of a sport for them. They would mercilessly beat anyone they felt was out of line or "not behaving." It was not uncommon for them to simply shoot someone dead on the spot just for fun.

Women were raped and violated, with some camps even setting up brothels. During the Holocaust, approximately five hundred brothels were operated in the camps. The women who became pregnant were subjected to abortions. Many died from the procedure.

Gas Chambers

Early in the war, prisoners were typically shot dead by the SS in mass killings. As time went on, the SS realized they needed a more efficient way of getting rid of so many people. Thus, the gas chamber was designed.

Four gas chambers and crematoria were built in Birkenau in 1942. By June 1943, they were up and running. The crematoria could burn approximately 4,416 prisoners a day. If they ran every day, it worked out to 1.6 million people a year. For the Nazis, this was a far more effective solution than individually shooting each person.

During the first selection, the old, weak, disabled, pregnant women, babies, and children were almost immediately sent off to the gas chambers upon arrival. Those who were young, healthy, and looked strong enough to work were allowed to live, at least for the moment.

The Nazis were careful not to cause panic in the people since it would make the process less efficient for them. So, the people who were led to the chambers were made to believe they would be taking showers. The prisoners handed over their belongings, undressed, and entered the massive "shower." Once it was packed, the doors closed, and gas (Zyklon B) was piped into the chamber.

This photograph was taken at Auschwitz and shows a group of Jews headed toward the gas chambers.

It only took minutes for the prisoners to die. Other prisoners from the camp were then tasked with stripping any leftover valuables from the corpses, like gold teeth, and putting the bodies in the crematoria ovens. Sometimes, the bodies were dumped in a huge hole that was used as a mass grave.

There is no precise number of how many people died during the Holocaust. It is believed around six million Jews died, along with millions of other "undesirables." It is thought that one in six Jews died at Auschwitz.

Medical Experiments

Nazi concentration camps were also used to conduct medical experiments on humans with total disregard for human life.

There were three specific goals:

- To conduct research on how to best keep German troops alive on the battlefield or how to heal wounded troops;

- To test out new medications, surgical procedures, or make new medical discoveries;

- To confirm that the Aryan race was indeed superior.

Over seven thousand such experiments have been documented; however, the real number is likely much higher.

The cruelest Nazi physician was Josef Mengele, who was at Auschwitz. Known as the Angel of Death, he was particularly vicious and enjoyed torturing his victims in the name of medicine. He especially liked using twins as test subjects. One was used as a test subject, while the other was the control. The test subject was put through unimaginable horrors, such as being injected with diseases, receiving blood transfusions, or having their limbs amputated. When the test subject inevitably died, Mengele cut open the bodies to study the internal organs. The control twin was then also killed so they could be studied.

Mengele was also obsessed with eye color and collected eyeballs to study them. He hoped to find the key to ensuring that all Aryan women would carry blond-haired and blue-eyed children. Mengele believed that if this could be done, the world could easily be populated by the Aryan race.

He conducted hundreds of other torturous experiments. It is estimated that about three thousand twins were tortured at his command. Less than two hundred of them made it out of the camp.

When the war ended, Mengele managed to escape to South America. He died in 1979 without ever being prosecuted for his crimes.

The Brutality of the Camps

Concentration camps were made to sound like labor camps. The prisoners were led to believe that if they worked hard enough, they would one day be set free. The truth was most would never leave.

The actual horrors of the camps will never be known fully. When the Nazis realized they were losing the war, a desperate attempt was made to destroy the camps to hide what they had done. Camps were burned and razed to the ground. Some prisoners were killed while the rest were made to march to another camp. Many prisoners died during the Death March. The prisoners were just days away from liberation.

What we know of the camps is based on survivor stories, the remnants of the camps, and what the Allied troops witnessed and discovered.

Chapter 10: Fascism and Mussolini

What Is Fascism?

Fascism is a political ideology that developed after Vladimir Lenin's Bolshevik communists led a revolution in Russia and successfully seized power. The ideology spread in a number of countries between the 1920s and 1945. Fascism spread all over the world, including the Middle East, Europe, South America, Asia, and even the United States!

World War I was seen by fascists as a great social upheaval that opened the door to a new era, one in which liberalism was no longer relevant. Some viewed fascism as a radical movement that brought about positive change, similar to the French Revolution, while others viewed it as a violent, oppressive, authoritarian movement. Given that both Hitler and Mussolini were fascists and given the events of WWII, fascism today is viewed in the latter light and is seen as one of the causes of WWII.

Some of the key beliefs associated with fascism include:

- Strong emphasis on nationalism;
- Racial hierarchy and protecting the rights of nationals;
- The military's supremacy;

- Opposition to liberalism, democracy, and Marxism.
- Opposition to equality and individual rights;
- Rigid gender roles and the firm belief that women are lesser than men.

Fascism and Nazism share some common beliefs and core values; however, fascism wasn't nearly as extreme as Nazism. While fascists believed in a racial hierarchy, they did not possess the same hatred for Jews as the Nazis. Historically, Italians had always been tolerant and humane. So, in 1938, when the fascist government in Italy began to announce policies that were clearly anti-Semitic, most people were surprised. It is generally believed that Hitler's influence and beliefs swayed Mussolini.

In order for a fascist government to enforce beliefs and ensure obedience from its population, it needs to wield absolute control, which is why most fascist governments end up with a dictator who controls everything. In Italy, the man who led the fascist movement was Benito Mussolini. While fascism existed in other parts of the world, it is most closely linked to Mussolini because he was the first one to create a political party based on the fascist movement and stand for election.

Benito Mussolini

Born on July 29th, 1883, in Italy, Mussolini was likely destined to be a revolutionary from birth as his radical father named him after a revolutionary leader in Mexico, Benito Juárez. His family was very poor, and his childhood was hardly an ideal one. He grew up to be an aggressive and disobedient child who once attacked a classmate with a penknife. Mussolini was also a very intelligent child, and although he didn't excel in school, he received a teaching diploma and became a teacher.

After some time, he left his job and moved to Switzerland, where, like Hitler, he drifted aimlessly. But he read a lot of books on philosophy, ideologies, and theories. He began to gain a reputation as a good speaker and political journalist.

Mussolini was arrested numerous times for his views, and by the time he went back to Italy in 1904, he had already been mentioned several times in the Roman newspapers. For a while after that, he repeated the cycle of drifting, writing, and being imprisoned. During a lull in 1909, he fell in love and got married, although he was arrested soon after.

By this time, Mussolini was becoming fairly well known as "Comrade Mussolini." After his release, he continued writing in socialist papers before creating his own, *La Lotta di Classe* ("The Class Struggle"). The paper was incredibly successful and led to his appointment as the editor of *Avanti!* ("Forward!"), a socialist newspaper.

With the outbreak of World War I, Mussolini believed the government should support the Triple Alliance. His views on the war clashed with those of the Socialist Party, which was supportive of joining the Allies. As a result, he cut ties with the party. He eventually joined the Royal Italian Army and served in the war as a corporal. He stopped serving after being wounded and went to Milan, where he became the editor of a right-wing paper, *Il Popolo d'Italia* ("The People of Italy").

His new political viewpoints were outlined in this paper, which would essentially become the rallying cry of fascism. He wrote, "From today onward we are all Italians and nothing but Italians. Now that steel has met steel, one single cry comes from our hearts – Viva l'Italia!"[12]

Mussolini had been advocating the need for a dictatorship in Italy and began to drop hints in speeches that he might be the perfect man for the job. He slowly created a party based on his new political philosophy. Two hundred people followed him early on; this group was mainly composed of disenchanted and restless people looking for direction and people who wanted to create a new force. They were ex-soldiers, revolutionaries, anarchists, and socialists. The force was aptly named *Fasci Italiani di Combattimento* ("fighting bands").

Fascism in Italy was born.

It didn't take long for the strong, confident Mussolini to mesmerize the crowds. He was also visually appealing and quite

---

[12] Davis, Kenneth. *Strongman: The Rise of Five Dictators and the Fall of Democracy.* Macmillan Publishers, 2020.

striking against the backdrop of his supporters, who wore black shirts as a uniform. It didn't matter that Mussolini was sometimes cruel or that his opinions were not always based on fact. The people were hooked.

Inspired by Mussolini, fascist squads began to crop up all over Italy, attacking local governments and terrorizing socialists and the people. These acts were encouraged by Mussolini.

By 1921, the lawless fascists' control was spreading throughout the country. Mussolini planned his next step. Blackshirts (members of Mussolini's fascist squads), armed and ready for violence, marched to Rome. They wanted Mussolini to be appointed prime minister. King Victor Emmanuel III bowed to pressure, and Mussolini became the new prime minister. His party began a campaign of steadily undoing Italy's democracy.

Mussolini, in the meantime, began to merge his party with the military and established anti-union laws to protect wealthy industrialists. He promised them protection from socialism.

However, people from Mussolini's party felt they should move quicker. In 1924, Giacomo Matteotti, the leader of the Unitary Socialist Party, was assassinated. The time to take decisive action had come.

On January 3rd, 1925, Mussolini gave an address to Parliament, saying he was responsible for everything that had happened, indirectly implying he had Giacomo killed. No action was taken against him. Assured of his absolute control, Mussolini openly became the dictator of Italy, naming himself *Il Duce*.

Under his rule, Italy was a police state, and everyone was expected to obey him. While there is no doubt that big businesses benefited from Mussolini's rule, the truth is he did very little to help the regular people. They saw a continued decline in their standard of living, especially once the Great Depression hit.

Internationally, Italy wasn't as big an empire as Great Britain, the Soviet Union, or even Germany. Italy had a few colonies in Africa, which they promptly lost during WWII.

After Lenin's death, Mussolini and Stalin were on friendly terms. They had diplomatic relations but likely wouldn't have hesitated to turn on one another if the need arose.

As discussed previously, although Hitler would go on to greatly influence Mussolini and bring Italy into the war, Mussolini's first impression of Hitler was not positive. The two men eventually developed some degree of loyalty and friendship toward each other.

At first, Mussolini had no intention of joining the war, but he changed his mind in 1940, feeling that he had to stand by Germany. Italy's participation in the war was doomed almost from the start. In 1943, when the Allies invaded Italy, the people were ready to surrender and switch sides.

A certain amount of bitterness and anger had been brewing against Mussolini for some time, as they blamed him for putting them through an unnecessary war. By the time Italy surrendered, they were already plotting his downfall. Mussolini was partially shocked by how things had turned out but sensed that his time was up, readily agreeing to resign.

Within hours of his resignation, he was arrested and imprisoned.

As the war neared its end, Italian communists made the decision to have Mussolini executed. He tried to cross into Austria but was discovered and stopped. On April 28th, 1945, he was killed along with his mistress. Their bodies were hung upside down in Milan for the public to see. The swelling crowds celebrated the end of his dictatorship and the end of the war.

If we look at the evolution and eventual downfall of fascism, it is clear that it was an abject failure. Mussolini had nearly fifteen years to "fix" Italy and bring prosperity and happiness to his people, but he did not or could not.

Was Fascism a Failure?

Ideologies like fascism and Nazism promise great things to the people, preying on their weaknesses and desires. But in the end, the only people these ideologies serve are the dictators who thrive on total control and their entourage. They snatch power with the promise to help and empower others, but in the end, they do nothing for them.

One might have expected fascism to die out completely after the end of the war. While the original fascist regimes have more or less died out, fascist ideologies and ideas have not. They have simply morphed into a milder form. Countries like France, Denmark, Greece, and the United States have fascist parties, but politicians are (understandably) hesitant to openly describe themselves as such.

Chapter 11: Stalin's Red Wave

After the Russian Revolution in October 1917, the Bolsheviks' leader, Vladimir Lenin, came to power. The Russian Soviet Federative Socialist Republic was formed by the Bolsheviks, triggering the Russian Civil War (1918–1920) between the Bolsheviks (the Reds) and the anti-Bolshevik forces (the Whites).

During the Russian Civil War, the Whites were supported by major international powers like Great Britain and the US, but the Reds had a lot of support within the country and managed to win the war in 1920. Sporadic uprisings occurred until 1924. After the revolution, Russia became a communist country and was renamed the Soviet Union.

Communism is a political ideology that fiercely opposes ideas like liberalism and democracy. Communists do not believe in a class system or in private property. Under communist rule, everyone is supposed to be treated equally. No one should have more wealth than another, the basic necessities of life are provided to all, and everything is owned as a collective.

In short, everyone works in harmony to reap the same benefits and rewards. A capitalist, profit-based economy is replaced by communal ownership and control. In theory, an equal world sounds like a great idea, a dream come true for the struggling masses, but in practice, it doesn't quite work like that.

For communism to work, the people have to be governed by a totalitarian system. There can be no democracy. Because one person's actions may not benefit another, rights become restricted. There is the threat that exposure to other ways of thinking will make people want a different life, so the government imposes censorship. This way, the people only know what they want them to know. Finally, a country's economy thrives when people are gainfully employed, earning a living that they are then spending on material things. Material things are produced in factories, which provide employment.

Capitalism, while flawed, is a full circle that keeps a country running and boosts the economy. Communism is viewed as completely undesirable by developed, capitalist countries.

When Lenin died in 1924, there was a brief struggle for power. Joseph Stalin ultimately became the leader of the party.

Joseph Stalin

Stalin was born on December 18th, 1878, in Georgia (not Russia) to a very poor family. His full name at birth was Iosif Vissarionovich Stalin. He later simplified it to Joseph Stalin.

Joseph Stalin.

Stalin did not have a happy home life, as he was savagely beaten by his father. He learned Russian at school and was never quite able to get rid of his Georgian accent.

His mother wanted him to become a priest, but this would not be the path he followed.

As a young boy, he secretly read the works of Karl Marx, and at twenty-two, he became politically active. In 1903, Stalin joined the Bolsheviks and became an ardent supporter of Lenin. Slowly, he moved up the hierarchy of the party, proving his value, especially during the Russian Civil War.

Stalin held two ministerial positions in the Bolshevik government, which helped him gather a following. By the time Lenin died, the two were no longer getting along. Lenin was supportive of the quasi-capitalist New Economic Policy, with which Stalin did not agree.

Luckily for Stalin, Lenin died in 1924 before any lasting damage could be done to Stalin's reputation. He became the new leader of the country.

Under Stalin, the Soviet Union became a totalitarian state mired in class-based violence. The country did industrialize rapidly but at a high cost. Many beautiful historical relics in Russia were destroyed and replaced with statues of Stalin.

He ruled using fear and violence but developed a cult-like following, which was central to the idea of Stalinism. After the Great Terror, the people were so scared of him that they did not even dream of straying.

Stalin didn't make many friends in the international world either. He had a strained, distrusting relationship with the United States and tenuous diplomatic relations with countries like Great Britain. Russia and Germany always had a tense relationship. Fearful of a German attack, Stalin agreed to a non-aggression pact with Germany in 1939. He promised to turn a blind eye to Poland's invasion and even helped Hitler. In exchange, Hitler would stay out of the Soviet Union. Of course, Hitler broke the pact when it suited him to do so.

Stalin was a deeply paranoid man; he trusted no one, and it seems nobody trusted him. After the Germans invaded the Soviet Union, he was forced to work with the Allies in order to defeat their common enemy. But throughout all the discussions, no side fully trusted the other. The Potsdam Conference, where the leaders of Great Britain, the US, and the Soviet Union met, was filled with tension and suspicions. Almost as soon as the war officially ended, the threadbare relationship between the Soviet Union and the US fell apart completely.

And once the greater threat of Hitler was finally resolved through mutual cooperation, the Soviet Union and communism became the new threat, with the world entering the Cold War era.

Stalin's Great Purge

The Great Purge or the Great Terror is exactly what the name implies. Stalin led a campaign in which anyone he considered to be a threat to himself or his rule was purged.

He first got rid of members from his own party whom he felt were starting to turn away or were questioning his authority. Political opponents were his next target, and then the purge began to include regular civilians, peasants, minorities, intellectuals, scientists, and the list goes on. Basically, anyone was a target.

In 1934, a Bolshevik leader by the name of Sergei Kirov was assassinated at the headquarters of the Communist Party. The purge was launched after this and resulted in over a million people being sent to the Gulag camps. More than 750,000 people were killed.

Stalin's purge caused fear and terror to spread through the country, especially when he began killing without discrimination. He even had thirty thousand generals, officials, and troops from the Red Army executed! He was convinced they were planning to overthrow him.

It is estimated that roughly one-third of the Soviet Union's Communist Party was purged. However, the actual number is likely much higher, maybe even double, as many people simply disappeared. The Soviet Union was also known for hiding statistics.

The Gulag

And what about those who were lucky enough to escape death? Were they truly better off? Many prisoners in the Gulag have said they would rather have been executed than sent to the labor camps.

The Gulag was the government agency in charge of the Soviet labor camps. Political prisoners and criminals were sent to them. It was used as a way to politically repress the people.

While the Gulag labor camps were not used on the same scale or for the same purpose as the Nazi camps, the two forms of camps are comparable in how they were used and the treatment of prisoners. This is especially true of the forced labor camps. In both Nazi and Gulag camps, prisoners were starved, beaten, and worked to the bone, having to do grueling work for fourteen or fifteen hours a day. In the Gulag, the prisoners were given minimal tools and tasked with jobs like cutting trees or digging into the frozen ground. Some people felt so desperate they maimed themselves to become handicapped.

Nazi camps saw similar types of work. In both camps, prisoners lived in overcrowded shacks in inhumane conditions. Prisoners were often abused, shot, or killed by guards.

But the similarities end here. The Nazi camps' main purpose was to kill and exterminate a population. That was not the Gulag's purpose, even though most prisoners did end up dying.

The SS, incited by hatred and racism, made it their personal mission to kill as many people as they could. This was not the case for the guards in the Gulag. The Gulag did not have gas chambers or a crematorium. When a prisoner's prison term was completed, they were allowed to leave. Some were even granted early release for work well done. This did not happen in Nazi camps.

The Gulag housed the highest number of inmates during Stalin's rule. In the 1920s, the Gulag had roughly 100,000 prisoners. By 1936, there were five million! This number only continued to increase drastically until Stalin's death in 1953. A few days after Stalin's death, the Gulag set millions of prisoners free, most of whom were completely innocent.

Over time, the camps were converted into prisons. In 1987, when Mikhail Gorbachev came to power, he got rid of them completely. His grandfather had once been imprisoned in the Gulag.

The psychological, emotional, and physical trauma and horror endured by the survivors of the Gulag will never be understood properly by the world and continues to haunt and impact generations of Russians today.

Chapter 12: The Role of America

Historically, America's foreign policy was isolationism and non-interventionism. Its government had no desire to get involved with other powers, expand its empire on a large scale, or fight battles. Its focus was almost entirely on its own affairs. Of course, this is no longer the case, and this shift began partially with World War I.

When the Great War broke out on July 28th, 1914, it was very much a European war and problem. But it didn't take long for it to become a global war, with more than thirty nations picking a side. Most countries sided with the Allies, which was made up of powerful countries like France, Great Britain, Russia, Italy, and Japan. The United States, while privately siding with the Allies, remained neutral.

But as the war dragged on, it became impossible for the US to maintain its neutral stance. The war hit particularly close to home when a German U-boat torpedoed the *Lusitania* in 1915. The US ship had been carrying civilians.

Americans were outraged, and even Cabinet members were in favor of war, but President Woodrow Wilson continued to be cautious. He threatened war, and Germany promised it wouldn't sink passenger ships again without proper warning.

But in 1917, a telegram from Germany was intercepted saying Germany would be returning to submarine warfare and sinking ships with no restrictions. The Zimmerman telegram was the final straw for the US. On April 6th, 1917, the United States declared war.

Historically, it is believed that the US helped to turn the tide of the war, leading the Allies to a win and officially ending the war on November 11th, 1918. Its endless supplies of troops, artillery, equipment, and skilled commanders were a much-needed boost to the war-weary Allied troops who had been fighting for years. The Americans came like a vengeful force, defeated the enemy, and retreated back to isolationism.

And then WWII happened.

Interestingly enough, the events of WWII unfolded in a similar manner to WWI. At first, the US did nothing. It sided with the Allies but remained neutral until the war hit too close to home.

Pearl Harbor

The United States had already been experiencing some conflicts and tensions with Japan as the Asian country looked to expand its empire. Japan wanted to ensure the US would not interfere with its interests and wanted to cripple the US before it could make a move.

The direct result of this was the attack on Pearl Harbor on December 7th, 1941, when the Imperial Japanese Navy Air Service launched a surprise strike on the American bases located at Pearl Harbor, Hawaii.

An image of the USS Shaw exploding.

https://commons.wikimedia.org/wiki/File:USS_SHAW_exploding_Pearl_Harbor_Nara_8 0-G-16871_2.jpg

During the attack, 2,403 US personnel lost their lives, as well as 68 innocent civilians. Nineteen ships, including eight battleships, were also destroyed.

Without a doubt, Japan won this attack, but it would pay for the move dearly toward the end of the war.

In retaliation to the attack, the United States did the one thing Japan had hoped to avoid: the US government declared war and officially joined WWII.

Nagasaki and Hiroshima

By the end of the summer of 1945, it had already been a few months since Germany's defeat at the hands of the Allies. However, the war in the Pacific continued to rage with no definitive end in sight. President Harry Truman received warnings that if Allied troops tried to invade Japan to bring the war to an end, the number of casualties would be horrifying. Still, it was clear the war needed to end quickly and decisively.

After the start of **WWII**, fearful of what Germany might do, the US started developing atomic weapons. By July 1945, the first atomic bomb was tested in a US desert. By then, Germany was no longer a threat. But with this technology on hand, President Truman decided the best way to cripple Japan was to use the new weapon.

Before attacking, the Allies presented Japan with the Potsdam Declaration, which did not specifically mention the atomic bombing but did warn of severe consequences if it did not surrender. Although the US dropped leaflets about air raids before, they chose not to do so with the atomic bomb. It was better to leave the people in the dark and use this major shock-and-awe tactic to force a surrender.

The declaration was rejected. The American bomber *Enola Gay* was armed with one five-ton bomb, which was dropped on Hiroshima on August 6th, 1945.

The blast decimated the city. Over 92 percent of the city's buildings and structures were either completely destroyed or severely damaged. Between 80,000 to 180,000 people died at the time of the blast and in the weeks after from radiation poisoning, injuries, and wounds.

Truman told Japan that more would follow if it did not surrender. The Soviet Union even jumped in at this point, declaring war on the Asian nation.

There was no indication that Japan would surrender, so Truman decided to follow through on his threat. On August 9th, three days after the first bomb, a second bomb was dropped on the Japanese city of Nagasaki, but there was less damage because of Nagasaki's hilly landscape. Some key parts of the city had been shielded from the blast. The second bombing led to between 50,000 and 100,000 deaths.

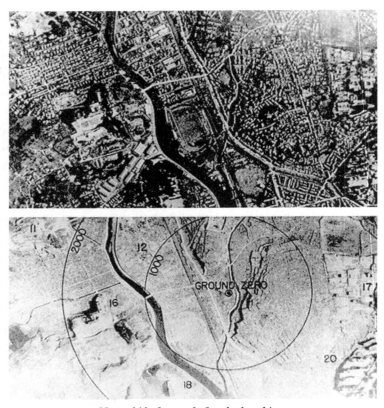

Nagasaki before and after the bombing.

*https://commons.wikimedia.org/wiki/File:Nagasaki_1945_-
_Before_and_after_(adjusted).jpg*

Several days after Nagasaki, Japan surrendered, and the war was over. Japan would formally sign its surrender on September 2nd, 1945,

Although many historians now believe that Japan was close to surrendering before the bombings, at that time, there was no indication that this was the case. After Germany's surrender, Truman believed the swiftest way of ending the war on all fronts was to knock Japan out.

His plan was not approved by all; Secretary of War Henry Stimson, General Dwight Eisenhower, and some American scientists objected to the dropping of the bombs. But Truman believed that if the war wasn't brought to an immediate end, thousands of American lives would be at risk.

The bombs were dropped without the approval of Congress, but Truman had the power to do it without their permission, so their approval was inconsequential.

While the bombs definitely had their desired effect, with Japan surrendering and WWII coming to a complete end, over seventy years later, many still debate whether it was really necessary to take such a drastic step. Unfortunately, whether Japan would have surrendered without the bombs is a question we will never have an answer to.

What we do know is that the bombing of Hiroshima and Nagasaki had long-reaching effects. Generations of people suffered as a result of the bombs. Survivors of the bombs and their offspring were susceptible to a range of illnesses, such as leukemia, blindness, and delayed development. It took Japan years to recover from the devastation. The bombings served as a warning of what could happen if there was another global war.

One could argue that the devastation and tragedy of Hiroshima and Nagasaki kept both the Soviet Union and the United States in check during the Cold War. Both countries witnessed firsthand what could happen if things got out of control.

The Marshall Plan

After the war ended, both the United States and the Soviet Union emerged as superpowers; however, it was soon clear the two countries were headed down very different paths and had very different goals. Stalin wanted the Soviet Union to expand into Eastern Europe and promote communism, while the US wanted democracy and capitalism and to stop the spread of communist nations.

Recognizing that the best way of stopping communism was to ensure that countries could stand on their own feet and improve economically, President Harry Truman signed the Economic Assistance Act, which allowed for the creation of an aid program in Europe. The Marshall Plan, as it would come to be known, would be one of the more brilliant moves by the US after the war.

The basic premise of the Marshall Plan was that the United States would provide financial help to Western European countries.

In exchange, they would need to find a way of working together and develop a plan that would allow economic integration between them. The goal was to stimulate economic growth and trade. The US felt confident it would prevent communism from spreading globally.

In total, the US sent over thirteen billion dollars in aid to sixteen countries. The money helped with investments, went toward the modernization of industries, helped reduce debt, and, perhaps most importantly to the US, ensured Western Europe was led by democratic, capitalist governments. The gross domestic product (GDP) in each of these countries grew alongside their economies.

The Marshall Plan set the tone for America's foreign policy and firmly established the country as a global leader and superpower. Many countries were grateful to the US, and there was also a sense of being indebted to the nation, which further cemented its role as a superpower.

Another outcome of the Marshall Plan was that it led to the beginning of the Cold War. Stalin wanted nothing to do with the plan. Under his direction, all of the Eastern European countries under his rule were forced to reject it.

With the start of the Cold War, tensions were once again high. The US maintained a strategy of "containment." Containment basically meant playing the long game. It meant being patient but firm, vigilant but conciliatory, and helping out countries that were resisting external influences.

The Cold War would last for four decades. During this time, both sides built nuclear weapons, knowing that one attack would signal the end of both countries. Although there were a few international incidents that almost came to a head, events thankfully never escalated that far.

Between 1989 and 1994, the Berlin Wall came down. It was clear that the writing was on the wall, and the Soviet Union and the Cold War officially came to an end on December 26th, 1991.

To this day, the United States is still considered to be one of the world's superpowers, yielding considerable global influence.

Key Figures f

Much of the United States' rea
the post-war world was shaped
brief look at four people who

Dwigh(

Eisenhower is best known to
of the United States. He als(
War II.

Eisenhower was born in 1890 and
His family had moved to the US from Ger.
ironic given the role he would eventually play in ac.
He served during WWI as a commander of a tank cr
unit and displayed great skills, although he was upset that he no
got to go to the front.

When the US joined the war, Eisenhower was assigned to work
in Washington in the War Plans Division before becoming the
commander of the American troops stationed in the United
Kingdom. He led the successful invasion of Allied troops in North
Africa, and in May 1943, he forced an Axis surrender in Tunisia.

Given this glowing track record, it's no surprise that after Pearl
Harbor, Eisenhower was tasked with creating war plans to defeat
Germany and Japan. In 1942, he was appointed as the Supreme
Commander Allied Expeditionary Force of the North African
Theater Operations. A year later, he was appointed Supreme Allied
Commander of Europe. This organization would go on to plan D-
Day (or Operation Overlord) and eventually liberate France and
Western Europe from German occupation.

As you now know, D-Day was a successful campaign. Through it
all, Eisenhower demonstrated fantastic diplomatic and leadership
skills and was greatly respected by his troops, his colleagues, and
global leaders.

In December 1944, Eisenhower became the general of the US
Army. It was a big honor and a significant promotion.

During the Battle of the Bulge, Eisenhower's strategic skills
helped the Allies counter the German offensive and send them

r finally ended, Eisenhower asked the liberating
horoughly document and photograph everything
the Nazi concentration camps. He had a feeling
uld attempt to cover up or deny the horrifying events
caust. Of course, he was right. And much of the
e see today of the Holocaust is in large part thanks to his

er the war, Eisenhower was urged by many people to throw
at in the presidential ring. He declined to do so and instead
epted the position of president at Columbia University.

In 1950, he took an extended leave from the university to take
on the position of supreme commander of NATO. He was given
command of the organization's European forces. Two years later,
Eisenhower retired from active service and finally decided to run for
president. He won and is generally seen as a popular president
today.

Franklin Delano Roosevelt

Franklin D. Roosevelt, commonly referred to as FDR, is the only
US president in history who was elected to office four times. He
guided the country through both the Great Depression and WWII.

Franklin Delano Roosevelt.

Roosevelt studied at Harvard and became a lawyer. His childhood was one of privilege, far removed from the realities of most Americans. Roosevelt's wife, Eleanor, who was also his fifth-cousin once-removed, and his fifth cousin President Theodore (Teddy) Roosevelt, greatly influenced him and opened his eyes to the plight of the American population.

He eventually entered politics and won a seat on the New York State Senate at the age of twenty-nine. As he became immersed in politics, he lost his air of superiority and was a great champion of progressive reforms. His health also played a significant role in shaping the man he would become.

When he was thirty-nine, he contracted polio, and for several years after, his focus was on recovery. He briefly removed himself from politics. In 1924, three years after being diagnosed with polio, he participated in the 1924 Democratic convention, his first political event in years. FDR felt uncertain about rejoining politics, but with his wife's help and support, he soon moved up the political ladder. Although it was challenging dealing with his disability, it made him a better politician. He was more relatable and sympathetic.

In 1932, he was elected president. He guided the nation through the Great Depression, earning him reelection. When WWII broke out, Roosevelt was careful to remain neutral, but privately, he felt strongly that the US should join the war. After the neutrality ended, Roosevelt did an excellent job of leading the nation at war.

Internationally, he worked hard to build a solid partnership and alliance with Great Britain, the Soviet Union, and other Allies. He helped supply over $50 billion of supplies to the Allied forces.

He also talked extensively about why America was fighting the war and gave the country and its troops a sense of purpose. FDR talked to the people he was leading in the fireside chats, which were radio programs that had started back in 1933. One of his most famous speeches, the Four Freedoms speech, stated the war was being fought for the freedom of speech, freedom from fear, freedom of religion, and freedom from want.

One of Roosevelt's most shameful and less than stellar contributions to the war was the signing of Executive Order 9066, which led to the displacement of thousands of Japanese Americans.

While Roosevelt led the nation through the war, he was unfortunately unable to see the final outcome, although he was pretty confident of how it would end. Struggling with poor health, he died on April 12th, 1945, less than a month before Germany's official surrender. He is often remembered as one of the greatest American presidents.

Harry Truman

When FDR died, his vice president, Harry Truman, became president.

Born on May 8th, 1884, Truman was the oldest child in a family of three. His father was a farmer, so he grew up on the farm. After finishing high school, Truman briefly became a banker before joining the National Guard.

When his father died, he went back to manage the farm, but as soon as WWI broke out, he volunteered for active duty. Truman fought in the trenches of France. After the war ended, he returned home and entered politics. His career continued to advance, and eventually, he became vice president and then president.

His two significant contributions to the war were overseeing its end and the Marshall Plan.

Truman also attended the Potsdam Conference and finalized the strategies to end the war. But after Germany's surrender, he needed to finish the war with Japan. Under Truman's orders, atomic bombs were dropped on Nagasaki and Hiroshima, leading to Japan's surrender. It was perhaps one of the most difficult decisions he ever had to make. Right or wrong, we cannot know. We know thousands of people died, but would thousands more have died if the war with Japan had continued? It remains a polarizing conversation today, and rightfully so.

When the Charter of the United Nations was signed in June 1945, Truman was there to witness it. Perhaps his biggest and most lasting contribution to WWII was the Marshall Plan, which was discussed above in greater detail. And, of course, Truman's biggest crisis after the end of WWII was the beginning of the Cold War. Truman won reelection in 1948, beating Republican Thomas Dewey; the election is still seen as one of the greatest upsets in US history. It was the last election before term limits were placed on presidents.

James Doolittle

WWII was peppered with extraordinary men and women who courageously fought for freedom and democracy, but there are some who deserve special praise. US Army General and aviator James Doolittle was one such person.

James Doolittle placing a medal on a bomb. This ceremony took place shortly before the April raids on Japan.

When WWI broke out, he was eighteen years old. He enlisted in the army and learned how to be an aviator and flight instructor. After the war ended, he continued his career in the US Army Air Corps, returning to active duty during WWII.

Several months after the attack on Pearl Harbor, he was tasked with leading air raids in Japan. It was a daring attack that required nerve and courage. The raid was carried out overnight on April 18th, 1942. Sixteen B-25 bombers dropped bombs over numerous Japanese cities like Yokohama and Tokyo. After the mission, the planes were unable to return to the USS *Hornet*, which was where they had taken off, because they ran out of fuel. They ended up crash-landing in Soviet and Chinese territories.

While the raid didn't cause significant destruction, it went a long way to boosting the morale of the American population. It also left Japan feeling spooked enough that it moved critical resources away from the South Pacific to Japan.

Conclusion

There can be no doubt about America's role in WWII. The country played a critical role and helped tip the balance in favor of the Allies. However, other countries played a significant role as well, such as Australia, Canada, India, Malaysia, and Kenya, among many others.

The Allies worked together to secure a victory; the win was not due to one country alone. However, we can deduce that America's support, diplomacy, and seemingly infinite resources, combined with cooperation between the major players, helped bring the war to an end.

Part Four: Key Moments

In this final part of the book, we will revisit a few key moments and battles from the war. But first, let's look at a basic timeline of the war from start to finish.

- January 30th, 1933 – Hitler is appointed chancellor of Germany.

- September 1st, 1939 – Hitler invades Poland. Great Britain and France declare war on Germany.

- September 1939 to May 1940 – Phony War

- May 26th to June 4th, 1940 – Operation Dynamo (Dunkirk)

- June 14th, 1940 – Paris falls

- June 22nd, 1941 – Operation Barbarossa

- July 10th to October 31st, 1940 – Battle of Britain

- December 7th, 1941 – Japan attacks Pearl Harbor. The next day, Great Britain and the US declare war on Japan.

- April 18th, 1942 – Doolittle raids on Japan

- June 1942 – Battle of Midway

- October 23rd, 1942 – Battle of El Alamein

- August 23rd, 1942 to February 2nd, 1943 – Battle of Stalingrad

- July 1943 – Allies invade Sicily.

- September 3rd, 1943 – Italy surrenders.

- November 1943 – Tehran Conference
- January 1944 – Siege of Leningrad lifted
- June 6th, 1944 – D-Day
- August 25th, 1944 – Paris is liberated.
- December 16th, 1944 – Battle of the Bulge
- March 1945 – Allies cross the Rhine.
- April 1945 – Russians reach Berlin.
- April 28th, 1945 – Mussolini is executed.
- April 30th, 1945 – Hitler commits suicide.
- May 7th, 1945 – Germany surrenders.
- May 8th, 1945 – VE Day
- August 6th to August 9th, 1945 – Atomic bombs are dropped on Japan.
- August 14th, 1945 – Japan surrenders. World War II ends.

Chapter 13: Barbarossa - Causes and Consequences

In some ways, Operation Barbarossa was like a pebble thrown into still water. The ripple effects of the campaign were far-reaching and eventually played a role in Hitler's downfall and Germany's ultimate defeat.

Hitler and Stalin had signed a non-aggression pact in 1939, so Stalin sat back as Hitler invaded Poland, believing himself to be safe from a German invasion. Therefore, it was quite the shock when Hitler reneged on the pact and launched an invasion of the Soviet Union, which was something he had been planning for some time.

Approximately three million troops (150 divisions) were assigned to invade the Soviet Union. The force was made up on 19 Panzer divisions, 7,000 artillery, 3,000 tanks, and 2,500 aircraft. It remains the largest invasion in recorded history.

Hitler divided his forces into three groups, with each group being given a specific task. Army Group North was tasked with taking Leningrad. Army Group South's objective was to invade Ukraine, while Army Group Center's main target was Moscow.

Hitler felt confident this would all be achieved in a matter of ten weeks. Their invasion began strong. In fact, on the first day, approximately 1,800 Soviet aircraft were destroyed.

While the Soviet Union had an enormous air force, none of their aircraft were very effective. They were unable to put up a serious fight against the far more powerful Luftwaffe. Within a month, the Germans were less than 350 kilometers away from Moscow. The efforts to capture Moscow continued until December 2nd, with the German troops a stone's throw away from the object of their desire.

But the harsh winter crippled the German troops, which were ill-prepared for the cold. By January of 1942, Germany was forced to concede that it would not be able to capture Moscow.

While Operation Barbarossa ultimately failed, the German troops *were* able to successfully blockade Leningrad, and it would remain under siege for nearly nine hundred days.

Operation Barbarossa wasn't a surprise to anyone who knew Hitler. The pact he had signed with Stalin was simply a way to give him some breathing room. His end goal had always included an invasion of the Soviet Union. Hitler's dream was to expand Germany to the east and gain a proper space (*Lebensraum*) for the German people. He intended to rid the Soviet Union of all its Jewish people, get rid of communism, and set up his own Nazi government. In his larger plans, Hitler's ultimate goal was to exterminate the Slavic people as well. To that end, millions of Soviet prisoners of war were killed by the Nazis. The only reason his larger plans did not come to fruition was because the Nazis were defeated.

Things did not go exactly as planned with Operation Barbarossa. The Soviets ended up being more resilient and powerful than Hitler had anticipated, and while the Soviet aircraft were not good, they had superior tanks. The weather also worked in their favor.

The Red Army did suffer some heavy losses, and the German troops did gain a lot of territory, but they were not able to eviscerate the Soviet forces or get them to surrender. Hitler's dream of taking over the Soviet Union failed.

And now he had made an enemy. The consequences of the operation would be quite high.

Enraged by Hitler's double-cross, Stalin allied himself with Great Britain and eventually the United States. Together, the three powers planned and strategized Hitler's defeat. When the time came, the Soviets crushed Germany.

As discussed in a previous chapter, the war could not have been won without the Soviet Union or the Red Army. Had Operation Barbarossa never been launched, Stalin would likely have joined the Axis powers, and the final outcome of the war could have been a very different one!

But Hitler did, and he failed. With Moscow a hopeless cause, Hitler instructed his troops to march farther into the Soviet Union to capture Stalingrad.

Chapter 14: Stalingrad - Causes and Consequences

The Battle of Stalingrad was fought halfway through WWII. After the failed Operation Barbarossa, another offensive was launched in June 1942 to destroy the rest of the Soviet Army and take control of Stalingrad.

The city was named after Stalin. It was an important city, as the Volga River ran right through it and was used as a shipping route that connected different parts of the country to each other. As an industrial center, Stalingrad produced many goods and products, including artillery. In short, it was an ideal city in a great location. And the fact that it had Stalin's name on it was a bonus that Hitler fully intended to exploit in his propaganda.

Hitler instructed his troops to kill all the men as soon as the city was captured and send the women away. Stalin ordered every Russian who was capable of doing so to arm themselves and defend Stalingrad.

The battle began on August 23rd, 1942. At first, the Soviet forces managed to hold back the Germans, but the Luftwaffe's relentless air strikes began to pay off. By the fall, the Volga River was rendered useless, the Luftwaffe was controlling the skies, the city was left in shambles, and tens of thousands of civilians and troops had been killed, wounded, or captured by the Germans and shipped off to camps.

The situation was getting increasingly desperate, but Stalin would not let his forces retreat or surrender. Reinforcements began arriving from other parts of the country, and other generals organized additional forces to launch a counterattack named Operation Uranus.

Soviet soldiers running through the trenches in Stalingrad.

https://commons.wikimedia.org/wiki/File:62._armata_a_Stalingrado.jpg

Through careful strategizing, the Soviet forces managed to wall in the enemy. The blockade meant the trapped troops had limited supplies. They began to starve and weaken. Things quickly deteriorated as winter approached. In the meantime, Soviet troops began working hard to break the lines of the Axis forces.

It was clear to Hitler the battle had failed, but he would not surrender. His troops continued to starve and die. By February 1943, the Soviets had taken Stalingrad back.

Roughly 100,000 German soldiers were sent to Soviet prison camps. A few groups tried to resist and continue the battle, but even they gave up in less than a month.

The victory for the Soviets and the crushing defeat for the Germans was a foreshadowing of how the war would ultimately end. Historians often point to this battle as the turning point for the war since Germany was finally on a downward spiral.

Chapter 15: VE Day

May 8th, 1945, was an important day. It was the day the Allies had been working toward since the invasion of Poland. It was Victory in Europe Day!

After six violent, bloody, awful years, the war was finally over in Europe. Hitler and the Nazis had been defeated, and the Allies had won. However, the war wasn't officially over; Japan still had to be defeated. But on May 8th, 1945, the people weren't thinking about Japan. They just wanted to celebrate their newfound freedom and their major victory.

People celebrated in the United States, Great Britain and its colonies, and the formerly occupied European countries.

At the beginning of 1945, the Yalta Conference took place. The Allied leaders sat down to strategize what they hoped would be the final offensive that led to the Nazis' defeat.

The Battle of the Bulge had been Hitler's last-ditch effort to regain some ground, but the Allies crushed him. In the meantime, Hitler's troops also had to deal with the Soviet forces on the Eastern Front. The Red Army was gunning for Germany's capital, and by the spring of 1945, they had attained their objective. On April 16th, 1945, the Soviets began their invasion of Berlin.

The German troops were exhausted and had shrunk dramatically. Even as the Soviet troops began to take over Berlin, Hitler, sitting in his underground bunker, refused to surrender, calling instead on every civilian, children included, to defend the capital. On April 20th, Hitler's fifty-sixth birthday, he came up to give out medals.

Soviet shelling began on the same day. Within days, less than 100,000 German troops were fully encircled by 1.5 million Red Army soldiers. The Germans knew there was nothing they could do anymore.

Hitler must have known the same thing because a week later, on April 30th, he married his long-time mistress Eva Braun and committed suicide. Their bodies were brought out of the bunker and burned to prevent any further indignities and insults. The Nazis were perhaps worried that Hitler's body would be strung up like Mussolini's and spit upon or abused. Shortly after, the Soviets secured the ruined and devastated Reichstag.

Red Army soldiers raise the Soviet flag in Berlin after its capture.

Germany's official surrender came on May 2nd, 1945; however, there were a handful of troops that continued to fight until May 8th.

In the weeks and months after, Berlin was in total chaos, with the Soviet troops reorganizing the city according to their desires and imposing their rules. Some Soviet troops treated the civilians horribly, raping women and inflicting other atrocities on the people. Other troops, however, gave out food and basic necessities to the people.

Meanwhile, the Allied troops were on their way to Berlin. American troops arrived on July 4th, 1945, and British troops entered the city two days later, on July 6th.

Given the situation, Germany had no choice *but* to surrender. It was a humiliating and despairing moment for the people. After initiating the war, after spending six years of fighting, after depleting all of their resources and losing millions of German lives, the end result was German troops on their knees begging the Soviets for mercy.

After the defeat and humiliation of WWI, this defeat must have been utterly demoralizing. In the short term, there were severe consequences to Germany's surrender. As part of the peace treaty, Germany was occupied by the four Allied forces. The country that had gone to war hoping to become a global power was now being run by foreign powers. Germany also had to pay steep reparations, which further crippled its economy.

However, in the long run, this was the best thing that could have happened for West Germany. After nearly fifty years of occupation by France, the US, and the UK, West Germany emerged as a powerful, developed nation. East Germany, unfortunately, was not quite so lucky. Falling under Soviet rule, East Germany's suffering continued until the end of the Cold War.

For the Allies and the world in general, Germany's surrender was critical to ensuring that democracy and freedom prevailed. Without timely Allied intervention, without the Marshall Plan, and without the defeat of Japan, would most of the world be enjoying the type of life that we do today? Or would fascism and communism have spread throughout the world, becoming the dominant ideology?

One thing is for sure, without Germany's defeat, the world would have looked very different today.

Fun Facts – Hitler's Death

It's hard to imagine that there could be any such thing as a fun fact when talking about WWII, but given the heavy subject matter, it might be interesting to look at a few random facts and myths.

One of the most common myths or conspiracy theories is that Hitler did not actually commit suicide. Seventy-seven years after Hitler's death, historians and conspiracy theorists alike still hotly debate whether he actually *did* die. Books, movies, and documentaries have been written and produced regarding this matter. Amateur sleuths and historians have spent years sifting through evidence and looking for proof to validate this claim.

It is believed that Hitler managed to escape his bunker and make his way to South America (like many other high-profile Nazi officers), where he lived out the rest of his life in quiet retirement. Some of the confusion stems from the fact that nobody credible saw Hitler's dead body. There is also some debate on whether he died by a self-inflicted gunshot wound or by ingesting poison. The lack of physical, visual, and concrete proof has given rise to wild theories.

Of course, there is no way to know for sure; however, there is no reason not to believe that Hitler died. One would think that, at some point, somewhere, someone would have caught a glimpse of him. Finally, given what we know of Hitler, was he really the type to simply disappear quietly and not seek the spotlight for decades on end?

Whatever the truth is, Hitler's death is one of the most persistent theories that still exist and will likely continue to exist.

Other Fun Facts

- VE Day, the abbreviation for Victory in Europe Day, was coined as early as September 1944, nearly eight months before Germany's surrender, because the Allies felt confident that they would win the war.

- In the movies, surrendering to an enemy is often portrayed by waving a white flag. Reality is not quite that simple. Finalizing the documents for surrender took over twenty hours to complete and was done days in advance of Germany's surrender. When victory was certain, cables were sent by **SHAEF** (Supreme Headquarters Allied Expeditionary Force) to world leaders telling them that Germany would likely be surrendering soon, and the documents began to be drafted. Comments, opinions, and changes from all parties took twenty hours to complete, and the document was finished at 2:30 a.m. on May 7th.

- On May 7th, 1945, a surrender ceremony was held in Reims when General Alfred Jodl signed the unconditional surrender of Germany. Stalin was not happy about this and made a fuss about the wording of the document and objected to where it was signed. He refused to accept a surrender that had been signed in France and insisted on a second surrender ceremony. This caused confusion for all parties, and some believed that Germany was still at war with the Soviet Union. A second ceremony was quickly organized on May 9th in Soviet-occupied Berlin. This means that in Russia, the celebration of VE Day is on May 9th, not May 8th.

- VE Day happened to fall on President Truman's sixty-first birthday. When Germany surrendered, it had been less than a month since he took office. It would be his first birthday as president. What a great birthday present!

- Hiroo Onoda was an intelligence officer from the Imperial Japanese Army who fought in WWII. He missed the memo that the war was over and was hiding out in the Philippines with three other soldiers. They carried out guerilla activities months after the war ended. In October, they saw a flyer saying the war was over, but they didn't believe it and refused to surrender. Over the next few years, many efforts were made to convince the group the war was over, but they refused to believe it. By 1972, Onoda was on his own; the other men had either died or left. He finally surrendered in 1974 (twenty-nine years after the end of the war!) when his former commander found him and officially relieved him from active duty. Now that's loyalty!

Chapter 16: Comparing Two Evils

World War I and World War II are often compared to each other. Both wars were triggered by Germany and fought by mostly the same countries. Both resulted in German defeats. And both were extremely bloody, violent wars that would have a lasting impact on the world.

However, there are many differences between them. How were the wars similar? How were they different? Was one war worse than the other?

Trench Warfare versus Air Warfare

World War I is closely associated with trench warfare, as most of the battles took place in the trenches.

With trench warfare, there is minimal mobility, with both sides digging deep, zig-zagging trenches. During WWI, the soldiers lived in the trenches for weeks since they offered some protection against bullets, artillery, machine guns, and poisonous gas (giving the soldiers time to put on gas masks).

Trench warfare was brutal, and nighttime attacks became the norm. If the initial attack led to a breach in the trenches, the enemy would then go around the trench to attack from the back while others attacked from the front, essentially trapping the soldiers in the trench.

Sitting in trenches for weeks while dealing with shelling and bombardments led to many soldiers developing PTSD. Physically, they were prone to becoming very sick from things like cholera, typhoid fever, and trench foot. Trenches were not sanitary, so diseases spread very quickly.

During WWII, the use of trench warfare was minimal; instead, there was a rise in air warfare. Aircraft had been used during WWI but were mainly used for reconnaissance. Due to the lack of mobility, it was important for planes to fly behind enemy lines to gather intelligence and draw maps. Later on in the war, planes began to be used to take out the enemy and conduct bombing campaigns. By the time World War I ended, it was clear to everyone that aircraft were the future of warfare.

Unfortunately, the next war came much quicker than anticipated. And when WWII started, air warfare really took off. Air superiority would become a deciding factor on who would win or lose.

Aircraft supported the ground forces and the navy for both the Axis and the Allies. Much of Hitler's early success was due to the Luftwaffe. Great Britain was saved from Nazi occupation due to its strong RAF.

For the Allies, air warfare was a huge support during battles. When the Americans joined the war, their technology and aircraft were far superior to anyone else's. Their planes played a key role in the Normandy landings and eventually helped the Allies win the war.

Machine Guns, Gas, and Close Combat versus Artillery and Modern Technology

Some of the most enduring images from WWI are soldiers trekking through the trenches wearing gas masks that make them look like aliens. WWI saw the arrival of new weapons, such as quick-firing artillery, or the development of old weapons that made them deadlier, such as machine guns, grenades, rifles, and mortars.

Armed with this slew of weapons, the war in the trenches was fought viciously with only one goal in mind: kill the enemy. Once the enemy managed to get into their rival's trenches, the combat turned physical, with soldiers fighting each other with whatever they could get their hands on, including shovels, knives, and clubs.

And then, to complicate things further, the Germans introduced the use of poison gas. The gas would be carried in metal canisters and then released to float toward the enemy. The gasses used early in the war did not inflict much damage, but by 1917, the Germans were using mustard gas. Mustard gas attacks the skin and leads to blindness. It is lethal, and the gas masks offered very little protection against it. Sadly, the victims who survived would go on to suffer from the effects of the gas for the rest of their lives.

During WWII, the Nazis accidentally developed a gas called sarin. They had enough to kill millions of people, and high-ranking Nazi officials wanted Hitler to give the go-ahead to unleash the gas. But for whatever reason, Hitler didn't want to. We'll never know his reason for not doing so, but many historians believe he didn't want to because he himself had been a victim of a mustard gas attack during WWI.

Instead of gas, WWII was fought with artillery units and modern technology. The main weapon of choice for the infantry was the M1 Garand, a semi-automatic rifle that was easy to use, light to carry, and very deadly. Machine guns, grenades, flamethrowers, and submachine guns were also used.

Like WWI, tanks were also used. However, WWII introduced new technologies, such as radar systems, computers, penicillin, and the atomic bomb. The atomic bomb led to Japan's surrender, bringing the war to an end.

Death Tolls

Both wars resulted in massive casualties, but the death toll in World War II was significantly higher.

During WWI, an estimated forty-six million people were affected directly by the war.

- 10 million military troops died.

- 7 million civilians died.

- 21 million people were wounded or injured.

- 8 million people went missing or were imprisoned.

In contrast, the estimated death tolls for WWII vary between fifty and eighty million people.

- 20 million military troops died.

- 38 to 45 million civilians died (from injuries, mass bombings, or other war-related diseases).
- 11 million deaths as a result of Nazi extermination programs.
- 3.6 million deaths in Soviet Gulag.

These are just estimates; the true numbers will never be known.

WWII wiped out over 3 percent of the world's population. It is the deadliest military conflict in recorded history (likely in all of history) and far surpasses WWI's death toll.

Conclusion

It is said we must learn from the past, that we must learn from history.

What did World War II teach us? Millions of lives were lost and destroyed during the war. Millions more became displaced refugees, losing their homes and identities. Countries and cities were ravaged, becoming ruins.

When we look around at the world we live in today and reflect back on the events and tragedies of this war that happened not even a century ago, was it worth it? Or was it all for nothing? What did the world gain?

There is perhaps no single answer to that question because what the world gained depends on your viewpoint and likely where you live in the world.

Regardless of what one personally thinks, the cost of the war was great. The sacrifices made were enormous. The genocide that was perpetrated is a black mark in history, and sadly enough, sentiments that brought about the rise of Hitler are still being touted today.

Based on numbers alone, WWII is definitely the bloodiest war in recorded history. It reshaped the world and changed the old way of doing things, ushering in a new era of foreign policy, diplomatic relations, and the rise of capitalist democracies.

Prior to WWII, many countries, like the United States, practiced isolationism. The war changed the global landscape, making isolationism impossible. Countries had to work together and maintain ties in a way they never had to do before. Many of these ties still exist today through global or regional organizations like NATO.

Without a doubt, World War II changed the face of the world. It is hard to imagine what would have happened if Hitler had succeeded. Thankfully, we will never know, but it is important to remember what happened during this war. People often say history repeats itself, but this is one event that should never be repeated.

Here's another book by Enthralling History that you might like

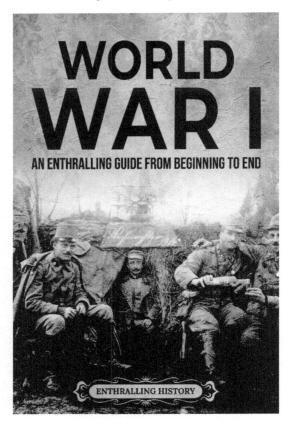

Free limited time bonus

Stop for a moment. We have a free bonus set up for you. The problem is this: we forget 90% of everything that we read after 7 days. Crazy fact, right? Here's the solution: we've created a printable, 1-page pdf summary for this book that you're reading now. All you have to do to get your free pdf summary is to go to the following website: **https://livetolearn.lpages.co/enthrallinghistory/**

Once you do, it will be intuitive. Enjoy, and thank you!

Sources

Burkham, Thomas W. "League of Nations and Japan."
Encyclopedia 1914-1918. 10 June 2021. https://encyclopedia.1914-1918-online.net/article/league_of_nations_and_japan#:~:text=The%20Assembly%2C%20by%20a%20vote,from%20the%20League%20of%20Nations.

Swift, John. "Mukden Incident."
Britannica. https://www.britannica.com/event/Mukden-Incident

"Leaders and Controversies."
The National Archives.
https://www.nationalarchives.gov.uk/education/leaders-and-controversies/g3/cs1/#:~:text=A%20year%20earlier%20Mussolini%20had,Mussolini%20demanded%20an%20apology.

A&E Television Networks. "German General Erwin Rommel Arrives in Africa."
History. 10 February 2020. https://www.history.com/this-day-in-history/rommel-in-africa

National Army Museum. "Second World War - Battle of El-Alamein."
NAM. https://www.nam.ac.uk/explore/battle-alamein

Jeff Wallenfeldt. "Atlantic Charter."
Britannica. 7 August 2022. https://www.britannica.com/event/Atlantic-Charter

Office of the Historian. "The Atlantic Conference and Charter, 1941."
https://history.state.gov/milestones/1937-1945/atlantic-conf

Jennifer Llewellyn, Jim Southey, Steve Thompson. "Hitler and Mussolini."
Alpha History. 26 August 2015.
https://alphahistory.com/nazigermany/hitler-and-mussolini/

Tharoor, Ishaan. "Don't forget how the Soviet Union saved the world from Hitler."
Washington Post. 8 May 2015.

https://www.washingtonpost.com/news/worldviews/wp/2015/05/08/dont-forget-how-the-soviet-union-saved-the-world-from-hitler/

History Stories. "How D-Day Changed the Course of WWII." https://www.history.com/news/d-day-important-world-war-ii-victory

Italy Since 1945. "The First Decades after World War II." Britannica. https://www.britannica.com/place/Italy/Italy-since-1945

Occupation and Reconstruction of Japan, 1945–52. https://history.state.gov/milestones/1945-1952/japan-reconstruction#:~:text=After%20the%20defeat%20of%20Japan,%2C%20economic%2C%20and%20social%20reforms

Wikipedia. "German Casualties in World War II." https://en.wikipedia.org/wiki/German_casualties_in_World_War_II

BBC. "How Britain lost an empire – war and government." BBC Bitesize. https://www.bbc.co.uk/bitesize/guides/zyh9ycw/revision/4#:~:text=World%20War%20Two%20had%20been,the%20rebuilding%20of%20the%20country.

Kids Britannica. "British Decolonization in Africa." https://kids.britannica.com/students/article/British-Decolonization-in-Africa/310389

Goodwin, Doris. "The Way We Won: America's Economic Breakthrough during World War II." The American Prospect. 19 December 2001. https://prospect.org/health/way-won-america-s-economic-breakthrough-world-war-ii/

The Man Behind Hitler. "World War II Propaganda." PBS. https://www.pbs.org/wgbh/americanexperience/features/goebbels-propaganda/

D Day – Eyewitness Accounts of WWII. https://www.normandy1944.info/home/battles

Holzwarth, Larry. "A Day in the Life of an Infantry-Man in World War II." American History. 14 July 2018. https://historycollection.com/a-day-in-the-life-of-an-infantry-man-in-world-war-ii/10/

Whitman, John. "Japan's Fatally Flawed Air Forces in World War II." HistoryNet. 28 July 2006. https://www.historynet.com/japans-fatally-flawed-air-forces-in-world-war-ii-2/

Imperial War Museum. "RAF Bomber Command during the Second World War."
https://www.iwm.org.uk/history/raf-bomber-command-during-the-second-world-war#:~:text=The%20Royal%20Air%20Force's%20(RAF,strategy%20for%20winning%20the%20war.

The History Place. "The Rise of Adolf Hitler."
https://www.historyplace.com/worldwar2/riseofhitler/warone.htm

United States Holocaust Memorial Museum. "Prisoner bunk bed from Auschwitz concentration camp."
https://collections.ushmm.org/search/catalog/irn94891

Auschwitz-Birkenau. https://www.auschwitz.org/en/history/life-in-the-camp/

Holocaust Encyclopedia. "At the Killing Centers."
https://encyclopedia.ushmm.org/content/en/article/at-the-killing-centers

A&E Television Networks. "Gulag."
History. 17 August 2022.
https://www.history.com/topics/russia/gulag#:~:text=Conditions%20at%20the%20Gulag%20were,still%20permeates%20Russian%20society%20today.

Campaign for Nuclear Disarmament. "Hiroshima and Nagasaki."
https://cnduk.org/resources/hiroshima-and-nagasaki/#:~:text=Almost%2063%25%20of%20the%20buildings,of%20a%20population%20of%20350%2C000.

World War II. "Timeline of World War II."
https://wwiifoundation.org/timeline-of-wwii/

The National WWII Museum. "Worldwide Deaths in World War II."
https://www.nationalww2museum.org/students-teachers/student-resources/research-starters/research-starters-worldwide-deaths-world-war

Canadian War Museum. "Canada and the First World War."
https://www.warmuseum.ca/firstworldwar/history/battles-and-fighting/weapons-on-land/poison-gas/

The National WWII Museum. "The Cost of Victory."
https://www.nationalww2museum.org/war/articles/cost-victory

Wikipedia. "World War II."
https://en.wikipedia.org/wiki/World_War_II

Made in the USA
Coppell, TX
06 January 2023

10587995R00115